Brilliant
Home Networking for
the Over 50s

Greg Holden

PEARSON
Prentice
Hall

Harlow, England • London • New York • Boston • San Francisco • Toronto • Sydney • Singapore • Hong Kong
Tokyo • Seoul • Taipei • New Delhi • Cape Town • Madrid • Mexico City • Amsterdam • Munich • Paris • Milan

Pearson Education Limited
Edinburgh Gate
Harlow CM20 2JE
United Kingdom
Tel: +44 (0)1279 623623
Fax: +44 (0)1279 431059
Website: www.pearsoned.co.uk

First edition published in Great Britain in 2009

© Greg Holden 2009

The right of Greg Holden to be identified as author
of this work has been asserted by him in accordance
with the Copyright, Designs and Patents Act 1988.

ISBN: 978-0-273-72054-6

British Library Cataloguing in Publication Data
A catalogue record for this book can be obtained from the British Library

Library of Congress Cataloging in Publication Data
Holden, Greg.
  Brilliant home networking for the over 50s / Greg Holden. -- 1st ed.
      p. cm.
  Includes bibliographical references and index.
  ISBN 978-0-273-72054-6 (pbk. : alk. paper) 1. Home computer
networks. I. Title.
  TK5105.75.H64 2009
  004.6'8--dc22

                                    2008042266

10 9 8 7 6 5 4 3 2 1
12 11 10 09 08

Set in 11pt Arial Condensed by 30
Printed by Ashford Colour Press Ltd, Gosport

The publisher's policy is to use paper manufactured from sustainable forests.

Brilliant guides

What you need to know and how to do it

When you're working on your computer and come up against a problem that you're unsure how to solve, or want to accomplish something in an application that you aren't sure how to do, where do you look? Manuals and traditional training guides are usually too big and unwieldy and are intended to be used as end-to-end training resources, making it hard to get to the info you need right away without having to wade through pages of background information that you just don't need at that moment – and helplines are rarely that helpful!

Brilliant guides have been developed to allow you to find the info you need easily and without fuss and guide you through the task using a highly visual, step-by-step approach – providing exactly what you need to know when you need it!

Brilliant guides provide the quick easy-to-access information that you need, using a table of contents and troubleshooting guide to help you find exactly what you need to know, and then presenting each task in a visual manner. Numbered steps guide you through each task or problem, using numerous screenshots to illustrate each step. Added features include 'See also...' boxes that point you to related tasks and information in the book, while 'Did you know?...' sections alert you to relevant expert tips, tricks and advice to further expand your skills and knowledge.

In addition to covering all major office PC applications, and related computing subjects, the *Brilliant* series also contains titles that will help you in every aspect of your working life, such as writing the perfect CV, answering the toughest interview questions and moving on in your career.

Brilliant guides are the light at the end of the tunnel when you are faced with any minor or major task.

Publisher's acknowledgements

The author and publisher would like to thank the following for permission to reproduce the material in this book:

We are grateful to the following for permission to reproduce copyright material:

Ad-Aware screenshots courtesy of Ad-aware; Belkin screenshots courtesy of Belkin International Inc; BT Broadband.com screenshots courtesy of British Telecommunications plc; Google screen images provided by Google Inc.; ISPreview screenshot courtesy of www.ISPreview.co.uk; Linksys Images provided by Cisco Consumer Business Group. All rights reserved; Microsoft product screenshots reprinted with permission from Microsoft Corporation; Pearson screen image provided by Pearson Plc.; Speedtest screenshots courtesy of Speedtest.net; thinkbroadband.com screenshots courtesy of thinkbroadband.com.

In some instances we have been unable to trace the owners of copyright material, and we would appreciate any information that would enable us to do so.

Author's dedication

To my brother and sister.

Author's acknowledgement

The author would like to thank Robert Brent for creating exercises and helping prepare content for this book.

About the author

Greg Holden recently became a member of the Over 50s himself. He has written nearly 40 books on computers and the Internet. His books explore a variety of Microsoft Office products as well as how to operating an online business.

Contents

Introduction

Welcome to *Brilliant Home Networking for the Over 50s*, a visual quick reference book that shows you how to make the most of your home computers by networking them. It will give you a solid grounding on how to choose the right network for you, how it works and how to get the best out of it – a complete reference for the older beginner and intermediate user who is less experienced and confident working with the technology.

Find what you need to know – when you need it

You don't have to read this book in any particular order. We've designed the book so that you can jump in, get the information you need, and jump out. To find the information that you need, just look up the task in the table of contents or Troubleshooting guide, and turn to the page listed. Read the task introduction, follow the step-by-step instructions along with the illustration, and you're done.

How this book works

Each task is presented with step-by-step instructions in one column and screen illustrations in the other. This arrangement lets you focus on a single task without having to turn the pages too often.

Step-by-step instructions

This book provides concise step-by-step instructions that show you how to accomplish a task. Each set of instructions includes illustrations that directly correspond to the easy-to-read steps. Eye-catching text features provide additional helpful information in bite-sized chunks to help you work more efficiently or to teach you more in-depth information. The 'For your information' feature provides tips and techniques to help you work smarter, while the 'See also' cross-references lead you to other parts of the book containing related information about the task. Essential information is highlighted in 'Important' boxes that will ensure you don't miss any vital suggestions and advice.

Troubleshooting guide

This book offers quick and easy ways to diagnose and solve common problems that you might encounter, using the Troubleshooting guide. The problems are grouped into categories that are presented alphabetically.

Spelling

We have used UK spelling conventions throughout this book. You may therefore notice some inconsistencies between the text and the software on your computer, which is likely to have been developed in the US. We have however adopted US spelling for the words 'disk' and 'program' as these are commonly accepted throughout the world.

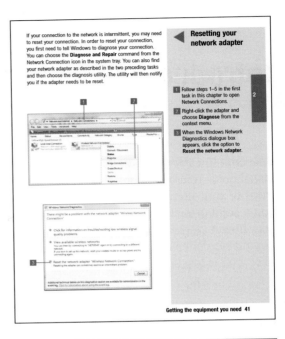

Networking for everyone

Introduction

You already know more about computer networks than you think. The moment you connect two computers to one another, you have created a network. When you start up your computer and connect to the Internet to get your e-mail, you have made a connection to the largest and most complex computer network around – the Internet.

If you have only one computer at home and you are satisfied with connecting to the Internet from a single location, you don't need a home network. But these days, one computer and one location just isn't enough. You might well have two, three or more computers for yourself and other members of your family. You all need to get online, and you all need to be able to share files and printers. Or you just want to be able to get online from your garden or another room.

Setting up your own network is a practical, do-able task and will have benefits for everyone in your household.

Even though you're not working in an office, you can create and maintain your own wired or wireless home network, and this book will show you how.

First, you need to decide on the best network for your needs and map out your network's topology. Next, you need to obtain the hardware you need, such as a modem or a Network Interface Card (NIC). Finally, you configure your network software, and connect each computer by following a series of well-defined steps.

Viewing your network

You purchased a computer, took it out of the box and plugged it in. Congratulations! Right now, your 'network' consists of only one computer. Each computer on the network is identified by its name. Believe it or not, your single, lonely computer has a name already. And you can view your one-computer network, too. To find your computer's name, you open the Network window. Once you have your home network configured, you'll use this window to view your other computers, which are identified by their names.

Open the network window

1. Click the **Start** button on the taskbar.

2. Click **Network**.

3. When the Network window opens, make a note of your computer name.

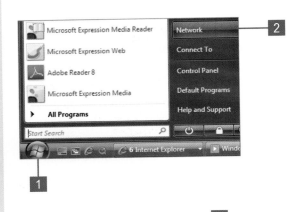

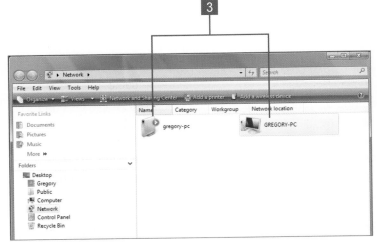

Discovering components of a home network

Component	Wired network	Wireless network	
Computer	Desktop	Laptop	
Network Interface Cards (NICs)	Ethernet card (PCI)	Wireless card (PCMCIA)	
Hub/router	Hub	Switch	Router
Cables/connectors	CAT-5 cable	Powerline adapters	

Viewing your network connection

Before you set up your home network, take a look at your existing connection: your connection to the Internet. You view the network configuration using the same tools you need to configure and manage your home network: the Network window and the Network and Sharing Center. Right now, you see only your connection to the Internet. When you have a home network configured, you'll see the other computers available in your home as well.

When you are connected to the Internet or another computer, the red X won't appear and the diagram in this window will show an active network connection.

Open Network and Sharing Center

1 Click the **Start** button on the taskbar.

2 Click **Network**.

3 Click **Network and Sharing Center** in the bar near the top of the Network window.

4 View your computer's name and the diagram of your network in the Network and Sharing Center window.

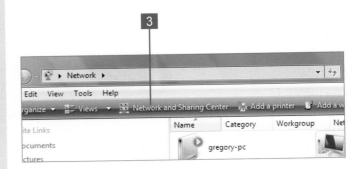

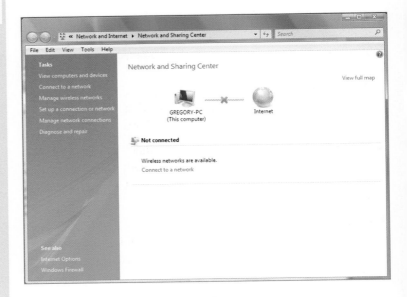

? Did you know?

You don't have to have an Internet connection in order to set up a home network. Although many home networks are set up in order for two or more computers to share an Internet connection, a network without a connection to the Internet enables computers to share data and other resources such as printers.

Understanding key concepts and terms

Some of these networking terms might seem a little technical, but their purpose will become clearer in subsequent chapters.

- **Ethernet.** A standard for high-speed communications between computers in a local network such as a home or an office.

- **Twisted pair cable.** The least expensive type of computer cable, in which two independently insulated copper wires are twisted around one another to reduce interference.

- **CAT-5 cable.** Short for Category 5 cable, which uses four pairs of twisted copper wire to connect computers in a LAN.

- **Client.** A computer that connects via a network to another computer that has been designated a file server.

- **Server.** A network computer equipped with software and/or hardware that enables the distribution of information to client computers.

- **IP address.** A number that uniquely identifies a computer on the Internet using Internet Protocol (IP). IP version 4 uses four-part numbers – four numbers connected by dots. A newer version, IPv6, uses six-part numbers.

- **Network Interface Card (NIC).** A card that enables a computer to connect to a network using Ethernet, wireless communications or another technology.

- **Router.** A network device that acts as a controller, directing and forwarding packets to different computers or other network devices.

- **Patch cable.** A specific type of CAT-5 cable used to connect computers temporarily, such as in a hotel room.

- **Local Area Network (LAN).** A group of interconnected computers located in a small area, such as a house, office or single building.

- **PCI.** Peripheral Component Interconnect, a standard for connecting peripheral devices to personal computers.

- **PCMCIA.** A type of card that uses the Personal Computer Memory Card International Association standard for data storage and transfer. PCMCIA cards are typically used by laptops for wireless network access or other functions.

Changing your workgroup name

Most home networks are part of a *workgroup*, a group of computers that are connected so they can work with one another. When Windows Vista is first installed, it creates the default name (yes, it's a little obvious) Workgroup. There's nothing wrong with this name, and you don't necessarily need to change it. But you might want to personalise the name to something you and the other members of your household can recognise more easily.

1 Click the **Start** button.

2 Type **System** and press **Enter**.

3 When the System window opens, notice the default workgroup name (WORKGROUP), and click **Change settings** under the heading Computer name, domain, and workgroup settings.

4 When the User Account Control dialogue box appears, click **Continue**.

5 In the System Properties dialogue box, click **Change**.

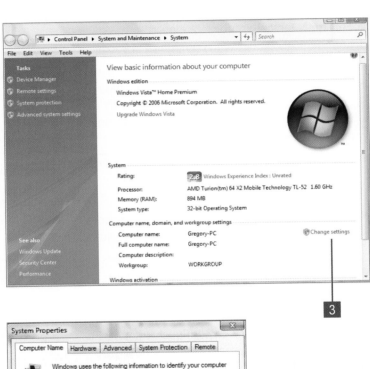

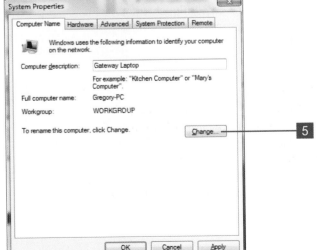

Timesaver tip

You can also change the name or enter a description of the computer you are currently using in the Computer description box to save a step later on.

Computer Name Changes

You can change the name and workgroup membership of this computer. You cannot join a computer running Windows Vista™ Home Premium to a domain. More information

Computer name:
Gregory-PC

Full computer name:
Gregory-PC

More...

Workgroup:
CORNELIANET

6

OK   Cancel

7

6 In the Computer Name Changes dialogue box, in the Workgroup box, type the desired name of your new workgroup.

7 Click **OK**.

8 When a dialogue box appears welcoming you to the new workgroup, click **OK**.

9 When a dialogue box appears informing you that you need to restart your computer to implement the changes, click **OK**.

10 Click **Close** to close System Properties.

11 Click the **Start** button, click the arrow in the lower right-hand corner of the Start window, and choose **Restart** to restart your computer.

For your information

In Windows XP, the default workgroup name is MSHOME. You can change the name as part of the Network Setup Wizard, which is XP's tool for establishing a network. Click **Start**, **Control Panel** to open the control panel, and then double-click **Network Setup Wizard**. When the first screen of the wizard appears, click **Next**. Follow the steps in subsequent screens to set up your network and give it a name.

Blueprinting your network, option 1: wired Ethernet

One option for connecting your home computers is to run wires between them. You can connect two computers to each other directly using a crossover cable. A more common configuration, however, uses a router to distribute an Internet connection among multiple computers. The router also allows computers to share files and to use shared resources such as printers. Most low-cost routers enable four or five devices to be connected using an Ethernet cable. If you need more devices in your network, you'll need to switch to a wireless router or use a second device such as a network switch. All devices that connect to the router using Ethernet need to be equipped with an Ethernet adapter, such as a card.

The big advantage of Ethernet networks is reliability and performance. Because you are using a hard wire to connect devices, your connection isn't subject to environmental obstacles such as walls or plumbing, or to other wireless devices. The big downside is the need to run cables inside walls and around your house in order to connect devices in different locations.

If you are setting up a wired network at home, mapping out the rooms where your computers will be and where your network hub will be is important. It's also important to decide where your Internet connection will be. Make sure you have a way to get to all computers from the hub. The hub will ideally be in a central location, in a 'public' room – in other words, a room everyone can access.

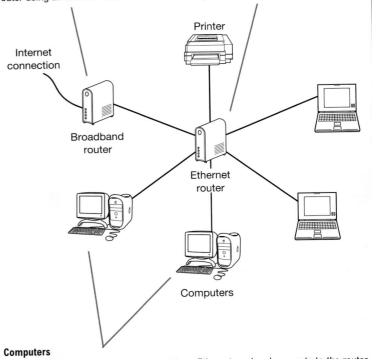

Broadband router
Your Internet connection comes into your house and goes to this device. The broadband router then connects to your router using an Internet cable.

Ethernet router
The typical low-cost router has five ports; one receives the Internet connection and the other four are used for printers, computers or other devices.

Printer

Internet connection

Broadband router

Ethernet router

Computers

Computers
Each computer needs to be equipped with an Ethernet card and connects to the router using a CAT-5 or other Ethernet cable.

Blueprinting your network, option 2: wireless

Wireless networks give you maximum flexibility and relieve you of the need to purchase cable and install it around your house. You can connect to the Internet or other computers using a laptop or notebook, and move from one room to another while maintaining your connection. You can even work in your shed or garden, provided your wireless router's signal can reach that distance. But wireless networks might not give you performance levels that are comparable to Ethernet networks.

If you are setting up a wireless network, you might think a map is irrelevant: after all, you can gain access from any place in the house. Right? Not necessarily. When you actually set up a wireless network, you begin to realise how things like brick walls and pipes affect your ability to connect or, at the very least, the strength of your connection. Try, if you can, to position the wireless router in a location where it will be relatively close to all the computers that will use it. If you position the router on the first floor, computers on the third floor might not have a strong connection. If you have a brick house or a very large house, or if you want to connect out in the

garden and you have a large property, make sure you purchase the router that puts out the strongest wireless signal.

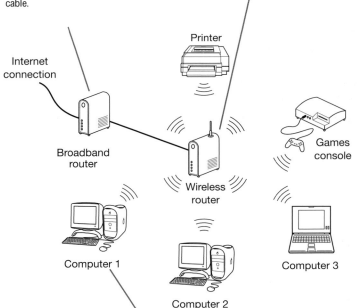

Wireless router
The typical low-cost router has antennas to transmit the wireless signal throughout your house, as well as several ports; one receives the Internet connection, and the others can be used for printers, computers or other devices.

Broadband router
Your Internet connection comes into your house and goes to this device. The broadband router then connects to your wireless router using an Ethernet cable.

Printer

Internet connection

Broadband router

Games console

Wireless router

Computer 1

Computer 3

Computer 2

Computers
Each computer needs to be equipped with a wireless LAN card to receive a wireless signal from the router. However, most wireless routers also permit wired Ethernet connections.

Blueprinting your network, option 3: hybrid

You can have the best of both worlds – mobility and performance – if you install a wireless router that also accepts Ethernet cable connections. The wireless router connects to the DSL, cable or other modem using an Ethernet cable. Then the router transmits a signal to any computer equipped with a wireless network interface card (NIC). For computers that don't have a wireless card, a conventional Ethernet cable can be used. If one wireless connection is weak, an Ethernet cable can be used to connect that computer as an alternative. For large houses or residences with far-flung computers, a hybrid network is ideal.

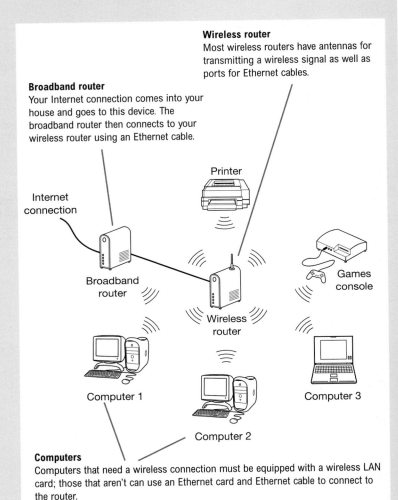

Wireless router
Most wireless routers have antennas for transmitting a wireless signal as well as ports for Ethernet cables.

Broadband router
Your Internet connection comes into your house and goes to this device. The broadband router then connects to your wireless router using an Ethernet cable.

Internet connection

Printer

Broadband router

Wireless router

Games console

Computer 1

Computer 3

Computer 2

Computers
Computers that need a wireless connection must be equipped with a wireless LAN card; those that aren't can use an Ethernet card and Ethernet cable to connect to the router.

Blueprinting your network, option 4: direct

Suppose you only have two computers that you need to connect to each other and to the Internet. They don't necessarily need to share your printer. You don't plan to expand your home network any time soon. And you don't need to work anywhere else in your home than the current locations of the two computers.

If all of these conditions apply to you, you don't need to buy a router, a hub or a switch. You can connect your broadband modem to one of your computers. Then connect that machine to the other computer directly using a crossover cable. You save time and money, and you are able to share your connection as well as your files with a reliable wired connection.

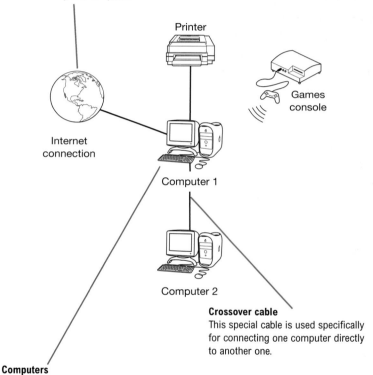

Internet connection
Your Internet Service Provider might provide you with a DSL or cable modem to bridge your Internet connection and your home devices. But if you don't have a modem you can connect directly to a computer.

Printer

Games console

Internet connection

Computer 1

Computer 2

Crossover cable
This special cable is used specifically for connecting one computer directly to another one.

Computers
The computer that connects to the Internet must be equipped with two network cards, one for the Internet connection and one that enables it to connect to the other computer.

Blueprinting your network, option 5: phoneline/hybrid

Wired connections generally give you a more 'solid' connection than wireless ones, but the problem is purchasing the long Ethernet cables that are needed to connect devices in different parts of your home. Wouldn't it be nice if the cables used to connect computers were already in place, having been installed before you purchased your home, or before you even moved in?

Enter phoneline systems, which use existing phone lines to carry data from one computer to

another or to and from the Internet. Phoneline systems aren't entirely 'plug and play' – you can't simply plug a router or computer into an electrical socket and expect it to work. You need to buy a special modem. And the quality of service might suffer if your phone lines are old or your phone connection is of poor quality. But you don't have to purchase and run Ethernet cables.

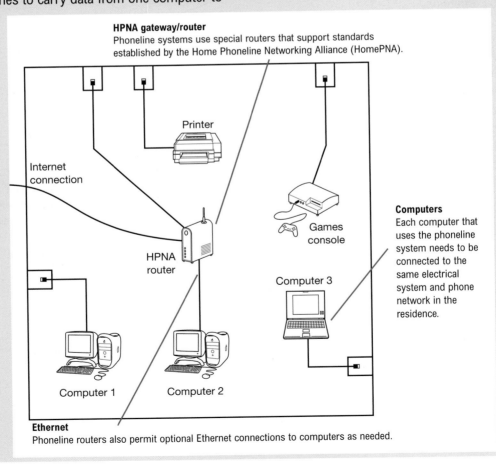

HPNA gateway/router
Phoneline systems use special routers that support standards established by the Home Phoneline Networking Alliance (HomePNA).

Printer

Internet connection

HPNA router

Games console

Computer 3

Computers
Each computer that uses the phoneline system needs to be connected to the same electrical system and phone network in the residence.

Computer 1

Computer 2

Ethernet
Phoneline routers also permit optional Ethernet connections to computers as needed.

Blueprinting your network, option 6: powerline/hybrid

Powerline technology is another option for using existing home cabling instead of having to purchase and install your own cable. Powerline systems use existing power wiring used to bring electrical power to all of your appliances to carry data from one computer to another or to and from the Internet. If you plug a powerline wireless adapter into an outlet, data can be sent to devices that are equipped with wireless network cards. This gives you the option of creating network connections over residential electrical lines for some devices while connecting others with wireless connections as well.

Powerline systems aren't entirely 'plug and play' – you can't simply plug a router or computer into an electrical socket and expect it to work. Each device on the network needs to have an adapter called a bridge to make it work. And you need to buy a special modem, too. But you don't have to string cables, and you get a reliable wired connection when it's all set up. This gives you the ultimate in flexibility: for remote parts of your property where wireless or Ethernet connections won't reach, you can use a powerline connection (provided you have an electrical outlet at hand and a powerline adapter installed on the device to be connected, of course).

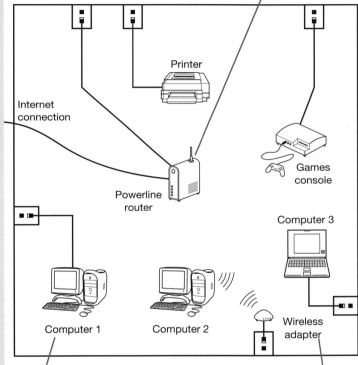

Powerline router
Your Internet connection comes into your house and goes to this device. The powerline router then connects to your electrical system through a wall outlet.

Computers
Each computer can connect to the network by plugging into a wall socket or by making a wireless connection. In each case, a different adapter is needed. For a wall socket connection, a computer needs either a USB to powerline bridge or a USB to Ethernet bridge, depending on which port on the computer is being used.

Wireless connections
For a wireless connection, a wireless card is needed, and a wireless powerline adapter needs to be plugged into a nearby electrical outlet.

Creating a client–server network, option 1: repurpose an old PC

Choose a computer

1 Find a computer that you aren't using or that you can obtain at minimal expense. Any computer with any operating system can be used. (This exercise assumes you are using an older machine with the Windows XP operating system.)

2 Check the available storage space by clicking the **Start** button on the taskbar.

3 Choose **My Computer**.

4 Click each of your drives in turn and note the storage space displayed in the Details box and in the status bar.

Did you know?

You need a computer with a substantial amount of storage space, such as 50 GB or more, to hold video and audio files. You might have to install a hard disk drive if you need more space.

Remember when you had to copy files over and over, moving them to floppy disks or other disk drives to get them from one machine to another? That's not only time consuming but also unnecessary if you turn an old PC or a hard disk into a file server. That way you can have access to the same group of files no matter what computer you're at. It's a great way to store photos you take with your digital camera or camcorder (not to mention your mobile phone camera), and you can view your archive anywhere.

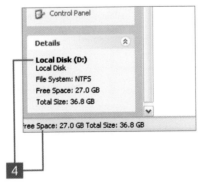

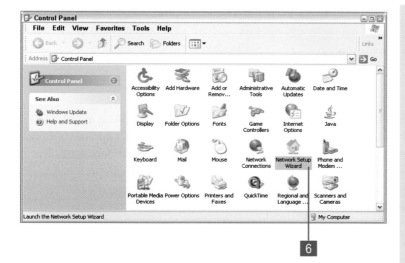

Creating a client–server network, option 1: repurpose an old PC (cont.)

1

Run Network Setup Wizard

5 Click **Start** and choose **Control Panel**.

6 Double-click **Network Setup Wizard**. When the Welcome screen appears, click **Next**.

7 Click the button next to Turn on file and printer sharing.

8 Click the button next to 'This computer connects to the Internet through a residential gateway…' and then click **Next**.

9 Name your computer and click **Next**.

10 Name your workgroup and click **Next**.

11 Click **Finish**.

12 Repeat the process on all of your other PCs, making sure you use the same workgroup name for all of them.

Peer-to-peer networks

Peer-to-peer networks are more practical than client–server networks, though less secure. In a peer-to-peer network, all the computers function as file servers, and all of the computers also function as clients – in other words, they all have the capacity to share with one another.

In a peer-to-peer network, there is no centralised file server, a single computer designated to hold all the files that the client computers need to share. Instead, each of the computers on the network functions as a file server in its own right. And each of the computers on the network can be a client as well. Each computer has a set of user accounts, and the users who have an account on a computer can access files on that computer. The files need to be contained in a folder that has been shared with the users who have accounts. The configuration is shown here.

In the diagram, the peer-to-peer network computers are connected to a central hub. Each is equipped with a network card, and each can share resources that are attached to it, such as modems or printers.

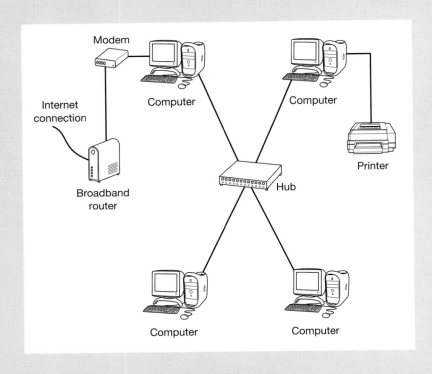

Once you have run Network Setup Wizard, you need to create a shared folder on your computer – a folder that contains the files you want to share on your home network. You need to set up a shared folder whether you have a client–server network or a peer-to-peer network. The shared folder can contain subfolders that keep your shared files organised. The primary difference is that on a client–server network the shared folder exists on the file server; on a peer-to-peer network, each computer has a shared folder that it allows other users to access. Another difference is the number of files you have to share and the range of people who can access them. In a client–server configuration, the file server is typically accessed by all of the computers on the network. In a peer-to-peer network, you may or may not share any files, and you may decide to share only with one person; the choice is up to the individual user.

Client–server networks are the types usually seen in office environments. In a client–server setup, a computer is set up as a file server. Its job is to provide access to the files stored on the machine by individuals who have the proper credentials (i.e. username and a password). The security feature makes them highly practical, and it's really the only reason you might consider setting up such a network at home. If you run a home-based business and your network will be used for both business and personal reasons, you might consider a client–server network. You hardly ever see client–server networks in home setups, and I mention them here only for the sake of completeness.

Setting up a shared network folder

1

Setting up a shared network folder (cont.)

1 Click **Start** and choose **Computer** from the Start menu. (If you are using Windows XP, click **Start** and choose **My Computer**.)

2 Click the drive or folder in which the shared folder will be contained.

3 Click **File>New>Folder**.

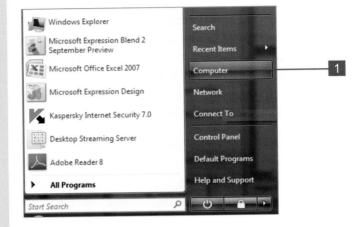

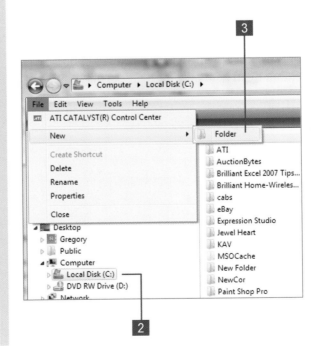

4 Type a name for the new folder and press **Enter**.

5 Right-click the file name and choose **Properties**.

6 Click the **Sharing** tab.

7 Click **Share**.

8 Click a user name if the one you want is visible, or chose an option from the drop-down list.

9 Click **Share**.

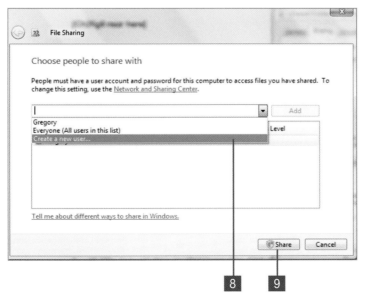

Creating a client–server network, option 2: use a hard disk

Obtain a hard disk

1. Purchase a new hard disk with a capacity of at least 50 GB. Look for one with built-in server software to function as a network file server.

Install a web browser

2. Connect the hard disk to your computer.

3. Go to the Apache website (**http://www.apache.org**) and download the latest version of this free web server that's available for your operating system.

You don't need to purchase a computer or use a second-hand machine to serve as a file server. Second-hand computers might have slower processors and less storage space than you like. An inexpensive hard disk can provide you with lots of speed and storage space without the overhead of having to find a fully fledged computer. If you use a hard disk, you won't have an operating system with built-in file sharing software. You need to set up software that enables the hard disk to share files. A hard disk doesn't include a built-in operating system, so there's no way to share files on it.

For your information

These days, you don't have to reuse an old hard disk to serve as a file server. Rugged, external hard disks with storage capacities of 250 GB or more can be found for as little as £80. Some, like the Buffalo HD-H250LAN, have built-in FTP servers as well.

Once you decide on your general network structure (client–server versus peer-to-peer), you need to decide whether a wireless or wired network will work best for you. This decision depends on a number of factors: your physical surroundings; the location of your computers; your need for mobility; and your ability to install cables and hardware. There's no perfect answer. You have to weigh the pros and cons, one at a time. One way to do this is to ask yourself a series of questions.

If you decide to go wired, you have three options: Ethernet, phone lines or a powerline network. The pros and cons are shown in Table 2.1.

Table 2.1 Wired networking options		
Option	**Pros**	**Cons**
Ethernet	More reliable than wireless	Expensive
Ethernet	Speed	Difficult to connect
Powerline	Easy to connect; no need to run special cables	Adapters and modem are expensive
Powerline	Flexibility: you probably have more electrical outlets than phone plugs	Older wiring and power usage can affect performance
Phone line	Easy to connect; no need to run special cables	Adapters and modem are expensive; need to install drivers and system components

Did you know?

If you plan on copying a substantial number of video or other large files, a wired connection is preferable because of the size of the video and other files you might be copying. You don't want your wireless connection to break suddenly while you're in the middle of copying a file or watching a video over the network. A wired connection will speed up copying and be more reliable.

◀ **Choosing your network type: wired or wireless?**

1

- How many computers do you need to connect? Do you plan to add more in the future? You'll have more flexibility and less installation work with a wireless network.

- Do you need to include mobile computers – laptops or notebooks – in your network? If so, a wireless network will give you most flexibility.

- What kind of operating system do you plan to use?

- Will all of your computers be on the same floor? Will they be close together? If so, a wired network will give you the best performance and reliability.

- Do you use cordless phones or microwave ovens? If so, they might interfere with your wireless connection, at least if they're on the 2.6 MHz band.

- Do you rent a small apartment and need your network to be easily portable in case you move? In that case, go with a wireless network.

- Do you plan to be in your home for a long time and are your rooms far apart? In that case, go with a wired network.

Creating an ad-hoc network

In an *ad-hoc* network, computers or other devices make a temporary connection for a specific purpose. Two computers might need to share files temporarily, or a computer might need to access a gaming device. *Ad-hoc* networks only exist in wireless networks; each computer that needs to make an *ad-hoc* connection needs to be equipped with a wireless card.

Make a computer-to-computer connection

1 Click the **Network Connection** icon in your Windows Vista system tray.

2 Choose **Connect to a Network**.

3 Click **Set up a connection or network**.

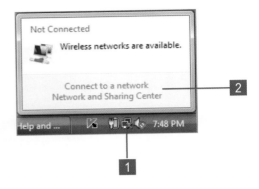

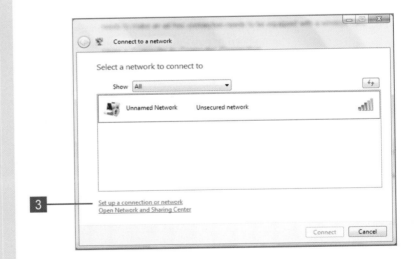

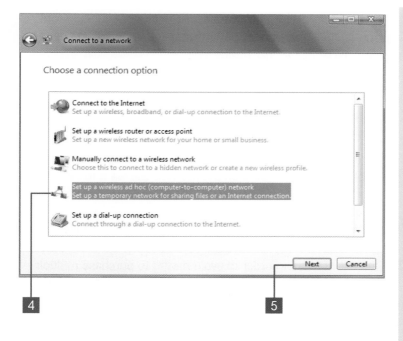

4 Click **Set up a wireless ad hoc (computer-to-computer) network**.

5 Click **Next**, and in the next screen, click **Next**.

6 In the next screen, type a name for your ad-hoc network.

7 Choose a security type.

8 Type a security key.

9 Click **Next**. In the next screen, your network connection is established.

10 Give your network name and security key to the owner of the computer you want to connect with.

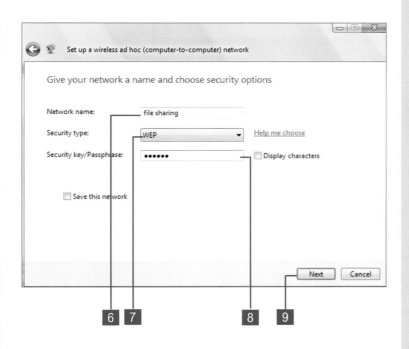

For your information

While you're in the planning stages, you need to take advantage of one of the alternatives to networking for moving files around. One of the easiest options is to purchase a small drive, called a Flash drive, that plugs into one of your computer's USB ports. You can copy the files to the Flash drive and then move the drive from one machine to another.

Deciding on the hardware and software you will need

One factor in determining the best network configuration for your needs is the amount of hardware and software you need to purchase or install. The basics include:

- a modem or hub
- cables to connect computers to the modem or hub or to wall connectors
- connectors – these will be phone line, electrical or Ethernet connectors, depending on the network you want to install.

Network adapters, also known as network cards, are also important. If your computers have Ethernet cards installed but none has a wireless card, you should seriously consider a wired Ethernet network in order to avoid having to purchase multiple cards. You should check your computer to see which kind of card (or cards) is available.

Check for network cards

1 Click the **Start** button.

2 Type **Device Manager** and, when the Device Manager appears in the Start menu, press **Enter**.

3 Click the plus sign next to **Network adapters**.

4 Make a note of the adapter cards you have installed and install any you need.

5 Click the **Close** box.

See also

When you configure a home network and multiple computers share an Internet connection, you need to make sure each of those machines is protected with a firewall. A firewall package (possibly for more than one machine) should be on your shopping list.

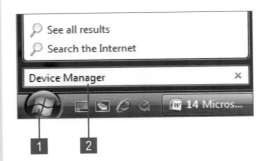

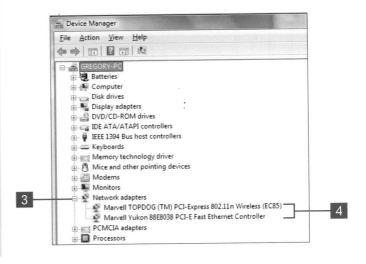

Dynamic Host Configuration Protocol (DHCP) is a system software utility that dynamically assigns network addresses to computers that are connected to one another. Just as every house on a street needs an address so mail can reach it, so does every computer on a network. An address is a combination of characters or numbers that identifies one device to another on a network. When Internet connections are involved, Internet Protocol (IP) addresses are assigned. DHCP is usually enabled by default, but in case it has been disabled for some reason, you'll need to enable it once again. If you're having network problems, it's always good to know how to check to see if DHCP has been enabled.

Enabling DHCP

1 Click the **Start** button to open the Start menu.

2 Right-click **Network**.

3 Choose **Properties** from the context menu.

Enabling DHCP (cont.)

4 Click **View status**.

5 Click **Properties**.

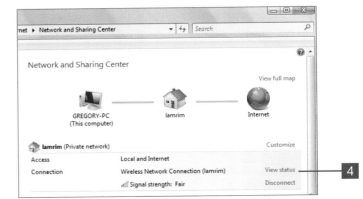

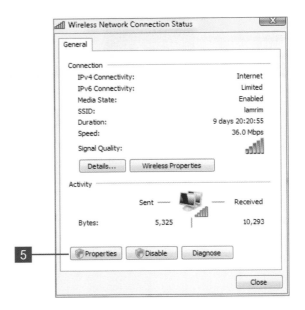

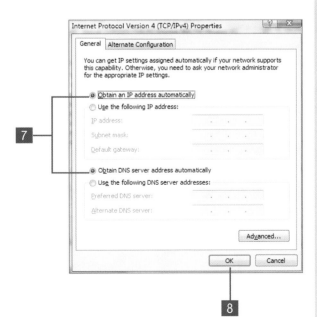

6 Highlight **Internet Protocol Version 4 (TCP/IPv4)** and click **Properties**.

7 Make sure **Obtain an IP address automatically** and **Obtain DNS server address automatically** are highlighted. This means DHCP is enabled.

8 Click **OK** here, and close any other dialogue boxes that are open.

For your information

An Internet Protocol address consists of a series of numbers separated by dots. Two types of IP addresses are typically used: IPv4 and IPv6 addresses. IPv4 addresses consist of four numbers separated by dots, such as 127.0.0.1. IPv6 addresses are much more complicated but are being used more often due to the scarcity of IPv4 addresses.

Getting the equipment you need

2

Introduction

In the first chapter, you were introduced to computer networking basics. You learned about different options for assembling your own home network. Once you have a general idea of the options, you need to start gathering the hardware you need. Every kind of digital communication requires hardware. Even mobile phones require you to have chargers to keep their batteries working and memory cards inside them to keep track of phone numbers and other data. And mobile phone towers keep the signals moving from one location to another.

Suppose you plan to go wireless with your computer network. You aren't going to be running cables from room to room, but you'll still need some hardware – and you'll need a bit of cable to connect your computers to that hardware.

The good news is that you probably don't need to make a huge investment. Chances are you already have much of the computer hardware you need to configure your home network. Most computers these days come with a substantial amount of equipment pre-installed. Taking stock of what you already have and getting your computers ready for network connections will make the rest of the networking process go that much smoother. This chapter focuses on the steps you need to follow after you decide what kind of network to install: checking your network interface card and router, naming your computers, and obtaining the rest of the networking gear you need.

What you'll do

Identify your current network cards

Enable a network adapter

Reset your network adapter

Get your home and computer network ready

Know the difference between routers, switches and hubs

Choose the right router for your needs

Understand what network standards mean

Choose a network interface card

Gather other networking gear you may need

Name your network computers

Identifying the network cards you already have

1 Click the **Start** button on the taskbar.

2 Choose **Control Panel**.

In order to determine which hardware you need to get your home network up and running, you need to do an inventory. The first step is to see which network interface cards (NICs, also known as network adapters) are installed on the machines you wish to network. If you purchased your computer recently, chances are you have some kind of card installed already. The available adapters might help determine what kind of network you want to create. If you have Ethernet cards installed and no wireless cards, you might want to save some money and set up an Ethernet network, for instance. If you are unable to connect to the Internet or to your local network at some point, it's helpful to know which adapter is being used so you can reset or repair it if necessary.

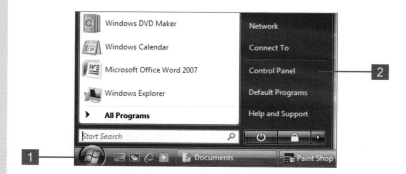

3 Click **View network status and tasks**.

4 Click **Manage network connections**.

Identifying the network cards you already have (cont.)

5 When the Network Connections dialogue box opens, click the down arrow next to **Device Name**.

6 When the list of your network adapters appears, check the box next to the first item on the list. The connection that is enabled by the adapter appears by itself.

7 Repeat this step for other adapters on the list and write down the results for future reference.

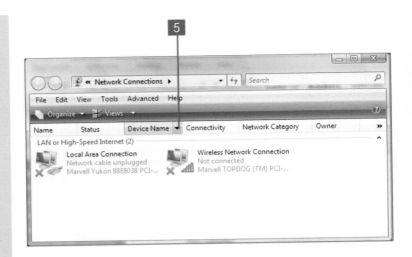

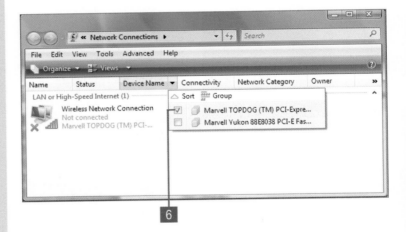

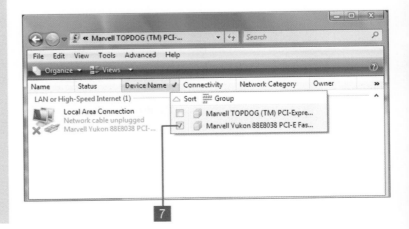

Once you determine which network cards you have, you might notice a warning sign next to the device, or a red *X* next to it. In case you cannot connect to the Internet, no matter how hard you try, this might be the cause: a red *X* means the device has been disabled. In case you find that a card is not functioning, you need to enable it. Unless there is a serious physical problem with the adapter, you should be able to accomplish this task yourself.

Table 2.1 explains the other context menu.

Table 2.1 Network Adapter Context Menu Actions

Menu option	What it does
Disable/enable	Disables or enables Network Adapter.
Connect/disconnect	Lets you connect or disconnect from the network.
Status	Tells you whether the adapter is enabled and connected and, if so, how long you have been connected to the network.
Diagnose	If you are having problems connecting to the network, choose this option and Windows will diagnose the problem.
Bridge connections	If you have more than one connection (e.g., a connection to the Internet through the Local Area Network and a wireless connection), choose this option to bridge the connections so you can use either one.
Create shortcut	Places a shortcut on your Windows desktop.
Delete	Lets you delete the connection.
Rename	Lets you rename the connection.
Properties	Lets you view the connection software that is associated with the adapter (for example, File and Printer Sharing or TCP/IP) and change it if necessary.

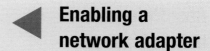

Enabling a network adapter

2

1 Follow steps 1–5 in the preceding task to open Network Connections.

2 Right-click the adapter that is disabled and choose **Enable** from the drop-down list. If you need to disable the adapter, choose **Disable** from the context menu (shown).

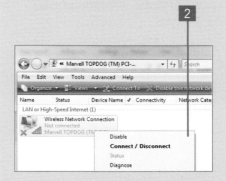

Resetting your network adapter

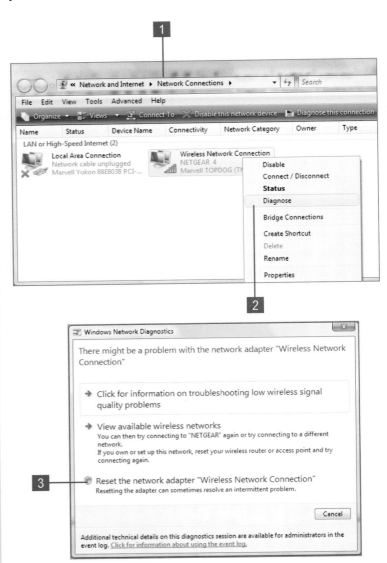

If your connection to the network is intermittent, you may need to reset your connection. In order to reset your connection, you first need to tell Windows to diagnose your connection. You can choose the **Diagnose and Repair** command from the Network Connection icon in the system tray. You can also find your network adapter as described in the two preceding tasks and then choose the diagnosis utility. The utility will then notify you if the adapter needs to be reset.

1 Follow steps 1–5 in the first task in this chapter to open Network Connections.

2 Right-click the adapter and choose **Diagnose** from the context menu.

3 When the Windows Network Diagnostics dialogue box appears, click the option to **Reset the network adapter**.

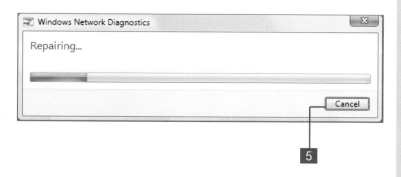

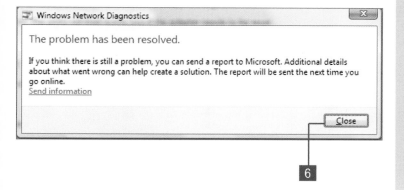

4 If a User Account Control dialogue box appears, click **Continue**.

5 A progress dialogue box appears; click **Cancel** if you wish to cancel the operation.

6 When a dialogue box telling you the problem has been resolved appears, click **Close**. The adapter will be reset.

2

Getting your home and computer network ready

A dizzying array of hardware options is available for configuring computer networks. Most of the hardware you need is specific to the type of network you plan to establish. But some options are important no matter what option you choose. Follow a few easy steps for making your home and computer network ready.

1. If you plan to set up a home power network, make sure all of the outlets you will use to connect your devices are on the same circuit.

2. Look through your house for openings between walls or floors where you can run Ethernet cable if needed.

3. Look for any metal items that might prove substantial barriers to a wireless signal, such as heating pipes or thick soil pipes, or cinderblock or brick walls.

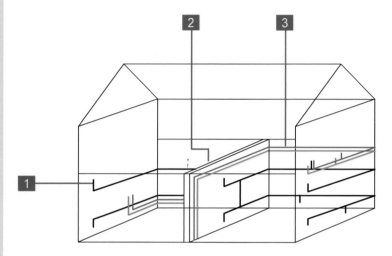

Comparing routers, switches and hubs

One of the key components of any network, whether it's at home or in the office, is hardware that routes packets of information from one computer to another, or from the Internet to individual machines. This centrepiece or 'core' of a wired home network can be one of four options, and they're each slightly different. Do you need a router, a hub, a switch or a network access point? The choices are less confusing than they seem. Here are brief explanations of what each one does:

■ **Hub**. A hub contains multiple ports that enable computers to plug into it with Ethernet cables. Hubs can only send or receive information at one time; they can't do both simultaneously. Hubs are slower than switches. They are the least expensive and simplest of the devices used to connect computers on the network. Wired Ethernet hubs support basic file sharing and connection sharing for home networks with or without internet service. Ethernet hubs support computers running any modern network operating system, including Windows, Linux and Macintosh computers.

■ **Router**. A router is perfectly suited to direct traffic between a local network and a wider network such as the Internet. If one reason for configuring a home network is to share an Internet connection, you will need a router. A wired Ethernet broadband router supports fast file sharing and connection sharing for cable, modem or DSL Internet services. These home routers integrate the functions of a traditional Ethernet switch, a DHCP server and a firewall for convenience. These routers usually cost less than equivalent wireless routers.

■ **Switch**. A switch has the ability to identify the destination of the data that comes to it. It thus directs the data to the computer that needs to receive it. Switches can send and receive information at the same time. Switches are more expensive and technically sophisticated than hubs but are well suited to networks that have multiple computers. Wired Ethernet switches support fast file sharing and connection sharing for home networks (with or without internet service). Ethernet switches support higher-bandwidth applications like gaming and sharing of large files. Like hubs, switches also support multiple operating systems. Although Ethernet switches cost a bit more than Ethernet hubs, switches are preferred for home networks unless minimising cost is the absolute top priority.

■ **Network Access Point**. This device is used only when you have an Ethernet network and you need to provide wireless access to it. You plug the access point into your router (probably through a USB cable) and can then join the network via a computer equipped with a wireless card.

Choosing the right router for your needs

The term 'router' is used here to describe any device that directs digital data from one networked machine to another. Unless you have a direct connection between two computers, you need some sort of router to make your network function.

1 Assess your network type and what you need:

- If you need to extend an existing network to include wireless access, you need an access point.

- If you need to connect two or more computers to the Internet, you need a router.

- If you need to save money and you have an Ethernet network, you can use a hub.

2 Choose the type of router that corresponds to the type of network you plan to create.

3 If you will create an Ethernet network, choose a router that has enough ports to accommodate all the computers you need to connect.

4 Make sure the router has the features you need, such as a clearly visible on–off switch or a reset switch.

5 If you choose a wireless router, make sure its antennas have the ability to transmit the distance you need.

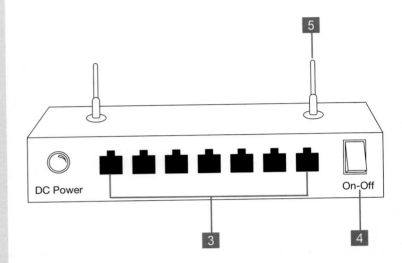

Network standards: what the numbers mean

When you begin working with networks, you see a variety of different number-and-letter combinations. Don't be intimidated by them: the designations tell you what kind of network data transmission system you're using. It's important to know what kind of network you're using so you can configure your software correctly and buy the correct add-on hardware if you need to. The main options you're likely to see are listed below.

Wireless standards

- **IEEE 802.11.** All variations on wireless LANs use this designation, created by the Institute of Electrical and Electronics Engineers (IEEE). The original specification only supported transfer speeds of up to 2 megabits per second (Mbps).

- **802.11a.** This standard supports data transfer of up to 54 Mbps, and is mostly used in business networks. It uses a higher frequency range than 802.11b – 5 GHz. Frequencies are regulated, which prevents interference from other devices, but means that signals don't travel as far, and don't travel as well through walls and other obstructions.

- **802.11b.** This standard has become widely popular with home networks. Devices that use it tend to be low in cost, but 802.11b has one big drawback: its frequencies are unregulated, which means that wireless 802.11b signals can suffer from interference from cordless phones and other appliances that use the 2.4 GHz frequency range. Your wireless connection can be broken when you get a phone call, in other words.

- **802.11g.** A newer wireless networking standard than 802.11a or b, this version combines aspects of both its predecessors. It provides for bandwidth of up to 54 Mbps, and it uses the 2.4 Ghz frequency, which enables signals to transmit with good range. But signals can interfere with cordless phones or other appliances that use the same frequency.

- **802.11n.** At this time of writing, this standard is the most recent. It improves data transfer speeds of up to 100 Mbps. But other signals can still interfere with it.

- **Bluetooth.** This protocol is used for data communications in personal area networks (PANs), which include handhelds, mobile phones, laptops and other devices that support Bluetooth.

Ethernet standards

- **IEEE 802.3.** All variations on Ethernet technology use this designation, including the original system, which transferred data at up to 10 Mbps.

- **802.u.** Fast Ethernet, which can reach speeds of 100 Mbps.

- **802.3z and 802.3ab.** Gigabit Ethernet, which can reach speeds of 1000 Mbps.

- **802.3ae.** 10 gigabit Ethernet – you can probably guess the speed limit here.

Other standards

- **802.16.** Broadband wireless LANs, which are intended for local and metropolitan area networks.

Choosing a network interface card

Why would you want to change the network card that's already installed on your computer? There are several reasons: perhaps the device doesn't work at all, the device works slowly, or the adapter is unsuitable for the home network you want. If you are in the position of having to choose a new network adapter, you can follow some simple guidelines. First, though, see whether or not your adapter is working correctly.

1 Follow steps 1–4 in the first task in this chapter, 'Identifying the Network Cards You Already Have', to open Network Connections.

2 Right-click the connection that uses the adapter you want to check.

3 Choose **Properties** from the context menu.

4 Make sure the message 'This device is working properly' appears. If it does, your adapter does not need to be changed. If it does not, you may need to repair or purchase a new adapter.

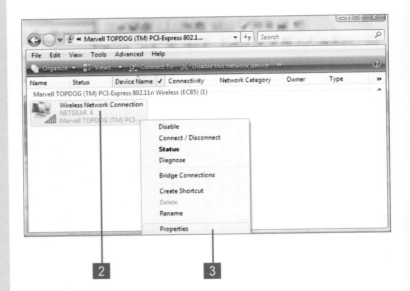

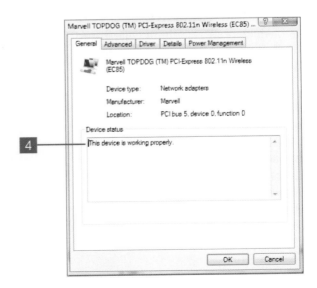

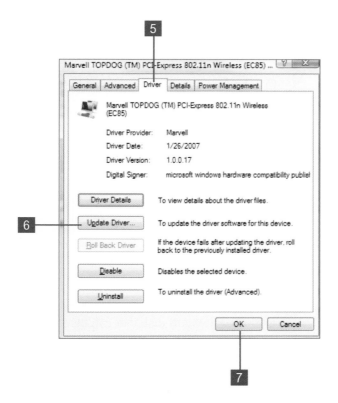

5

Marvell TOPDOG (TM) PCI-Express 802.11n Wireless (EC85) ...

| General | Advanced | Driver | Details | Power Management |

Marvell TOPDOG (TM) PCI-Express 802.11n Wireless
(EC85)

Driver Provider: Marvell

Driver Date: 1/26/2007

Driver Version: 1.0.0.17

Digital Signer: microsoft windows hardware compatibility publisl

Driver Details   To view details about the driver files.

6 Update Driver...   To update the driver software for this device.

Roll Back Driver   If the device fails after updating the driver, roll
                        back to the previously installed driver.

Disable   Disables the selected device.

Uninstall   To uninstall the driver (Advanced).

OK   Cancel

7

Choosing a network interface card (cont.)

2

5 Click the **Driver** tab.

6 Choose **Update Driver** to find a new driver for the adapter from the Internet.

7 Click **OK**.

8 If you cannot repair the driver and the adapter does not function, choose a network adapter that is made by the same manufacturer as your router. If you have a Linksys router, for instance, buy a Linksys adapter. They are almost certain to be compatible and work well together.

Other networking hardware you may need

When you're planning your network, you need to take all components into account. The number of networked devices you have might play a role in whether you need an Ethernet or wireless network, for instance, or whether you need a router versus a switch. Once you have the obvious components (computers and network adapters) accounted for, take an inventory of other devices you might want to add on to support your networked computers.

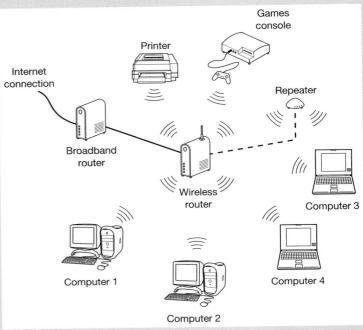

Add a backup device

You probably already know that your files should be backed up on a regular basis. (If you have endured a serious computer crash and lost data, you know this for certain.) A networked storage device can make the process go easily. Instead of having to back up each machine individually, you can use backup software that's designed to work on a network, such as Retrospect Remote, to back up files automatically.

Add network attached storage

A network attached storage (NAS) device is one that is added to a network especially for the purpose of providing storage for users on your network. It may or may not be used for the purposes of a network backup. Find a

high-capacity hard disk that can be networked so you can store data there.

Add a network repeater

If your home is particularly large or if you are experiencing network connection problems with a wireless network, consider adding a repeater. A repeater is a hardware device that extends an Ethernet or wireless signal beyond the current capacity of the current router. Network access points can function as repeaters when operating in 'repeater mode'.

Did you know?

Retrospect Remote by EMC Insignia Software is available at **http://www.emcinsignia.com**. A networked backup device is commonly known as networked attached storage (NAS).

When you send mail to a friend or family member, you need to put the recipient's name as well as an address on the envelope. Computers, too, need names so electronic data can find its way to the right destination on the network. Computer names need to be clear enough that everyone in the family knows which icon belongs to which computer. Those who give their computers names that are little more than 'inside jokes' might sound clever, but they make it harder for others in the household to use the network. If you need to change the name of your computer or another on the network, follow these steps.

Naming your network computers

1 Click the **Start** button on the taskbar.

2 Type **system** in the search box.

3 Click **System** when it appears in the Start menu. If an alert dialogue box appears, click **Continue**.

Getting the equipment you need 43

Naming your network computers (cont.)

4 Click **Change settings** under Computer name, domain and workgroup settings. If you are prompted for a password, enter it. If a User Account Control dialogue box appears, click **Continue**.

5 Click **Change** on the Computer Name tab.

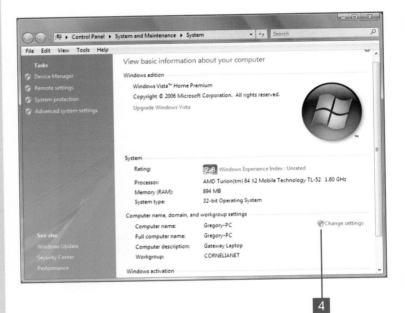

4

5

Naming your network computers (cont.)

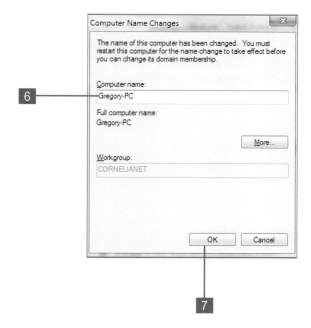

6 Type your new computer name.

7 Click **OK**.

2

For your information

If your ISP requires you to use a particular name for your computer in order to gain access to the Internet, don't rename it. Check with your ISP if you aren't sure whether or not to change the computer name.

Choosing broadband Internet access

3

Introduction

No matter how you old you are (and who's counting!), chances are good that the reason you want to network home computers is the need to share an Internet connection. The moment a second or third computer comes into your home, whether it belongs to a new lodger or a child or grandchild who comes to visit, you'll need to get those new machines online at some point. In order to ensure that all your computers can get online reliably, you need a broadband connection. *Broadband*, by the way, means that the connection's capacity to send and receive digital information (its bandwidth) is large or broad compared with slower connection methods like dial-up – hence the term *broadband*.

As other members of your household go online, you'll see your bandwidth increase. Some may want to view video clips online; others may want to download applications; and when your grandchildren visit, they'll no doubt want to do online gaming. A connection that's slow or intermittent will produce complaints and demands on you to make things better. Be proactive, and you can get things working smoothly up front. Some options for obtaining a good connection – or for improving the one you have – asre described in this chapter.

These days, for most of us using our computers from home, 'broadband' means a connection to the Internet which is leased for a monthly or annual fee from a cable television provider or a telephone or other company that provides Digital Subscriber Line (DSL) access. Both cable and DSL are far faster than old-

What you'll do

Check out your broadband connection options

Compare Internet access options

Reset your broadband modem

Check your distance to your local exchange

Get a better broadband modem

Test your current internet connection speed

Troubleshoot a broken connection

fashioned dial-up connections, in which computers literally dialled a phone number and connected to a computer owned by an Internet Service Provider (ISP) and thus got online. As difficult as it is for the younger generation to imagine, those connections were online only for the length of the phone call. Cable and DSL connections are now the way to go, not only because they are fast but also because they're 'always on'. For convenience and speed, they're the easiest options, and that's what you're looking for, after all. This chapter will present some easy-to-follow tasks designed to get you a broadband connection so you can get all of your computers online, no matter where they are in your home.

Did you know?

Of all UK households, fifty-six per cent broadband connections in 2008, up from fifty-one per cent in 2007, according to the National Statistics Omnibus Survey. In the South East region, seventy-four per cent of all households have Internet access.

You don't want to wake up one morning to discover that your ISP is offline or has gone out of business altogether. If there are problems with an Internet provider you're considering, you need to research that company beforehand. At the very least, you should be able to track its network performance to learn if it has had a lot of downtime or if customers are voicing other complaints about them. Start with the provider's own website, where you should be able to learn about service 'outages'. Then look for discussion groups, either on the ISP's own site or on other sites that track Internet access providers. Such groups will also help you upgrade to a better access plan if you decide to make a switch.

2

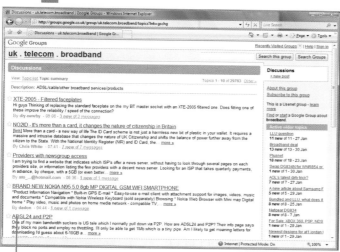

3

Checking out your broadband connection options

1 Go on your ISP's own chat boards and see what other customers have to say about them.

2 Scan the comments on sites such as ISPreview UK (**http://www.ispreview.co.uk**).

3 Try newsgroups; search Google UK.

3

For your information

The UK Broadband Internet Access page at **http://paler. com/uk_broadband_internet _access.html** contains links to Britain's most popular ISPs. You'll also find links to sites that compare prices and performance, and reviews of the major companies.

Comparing Internet access options

▶

1. Go to the Compare Broadband Service Providers page on the thinkbroadband website (**http://www.thinkbroadband. com/isp/compare.html**).

2. Check the boxes next to up to six providers you want to research.

3. Click **Compare**.

4. Review the graphs to compare the speed, reliability and customer service ratings for each of the selected providers.

5. Hover your mouse pointer over one of the bars in the graph to view detailed information about the ISP displayed. You may discover that a provider that has slower service has better reliability, for instance.

6. Click on an ISP's name to view more detailed information about the company.

7. Review the current packages available. Contact the ISP to set up a service if you can get a better deal than your current service contract.

Even if you are satisfied with your current Internet Service Provider, it pays to be aware of other options that are available. As long as you're focused on taking your computer skills to a higher level and getting up to speed with the high-tech generation, you might as well do a little extra research. Who knows? You may be able to get more for less. You may well discover that another ISP can give you more bandwidth and greater reliability, possibly at a lower monthly fee than you are currently paying. A number of websites in the UK compare fees charged by ISPs as well as their service.

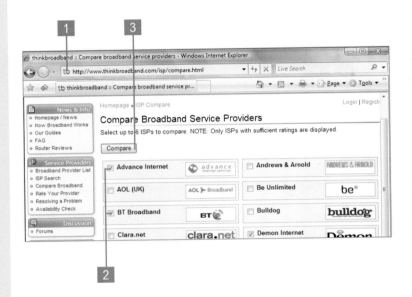

The good news is that you may already have an Internet connection. The not-so-good news is that if your connection is slow or intermittent with only one computer, when you set up a home network things are only going to get worse. But don't be discouraged. If you are having problems with your Internet connection, you may need to reboot your broadband modem. Chances are you'll be on the phone with your ISP's tech support staff and they'll tell you when you need to do this. But if you have lost your connection and you are certain you need to reboot the modem (for instance, if the lights indicating connectivity are out), you can do it yourself. If your modem has a reset button, the easiest option is to press it and hold it down for a few seconds to reset the device. If a reset button is not available, follow these steps, which apply to both DSL and cable modems.

Resetting your broadband modem

1 Unplug your broadband modem from its electrical socket.

2 Unplug your network router or hub from its electrical socket.

3 Wait about a minute.

4 Plug in the router.

5 Plug in the broadband modem and wait for the connection lights to go on.

3

For your information

What should you do if you're still not connected? You should reboot your computer and connect to the Internet manually. Alternatively, you should check your system tray to see whether a connection has been made automatically. How will you know it's time to celebrate? Your wireless or Ethernet connection icons should be lit up in blue if the connection is successful.

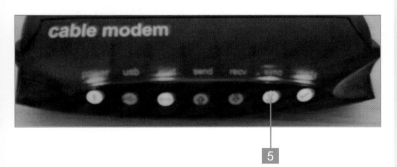

Checking your distance to your local exchange

1. Start up your web browser.
2. Go to to the ADSL Availability Checker utility (**http://www.adslchecker.bt.com/pls/adslchecker.welcome**).
3. Type in your phone number.
4. Click the **Submit** button.

Did you know?

You need to obtain your phone service from British Telecom in order to perform this test.

On a DSL network, your distance from your home to a facility called a *local exchange* can affect your connection. A local exchange, which is provided by your local phone company, functions as a switching station for phone lines in the immediate area. That allows your connections to be local although you're using long-distance services.

It's a good idea to calculate your distance before you sign up for DSL service. Be sure to find out your provider's distance limit. In the UK, BT Wholesale supplies DSL service and one DSL provider, ChunkyChips, recommends that you are located around 5.5 km (2.2 miles) or 3.5 km (3.4 miles) from a local exchange. But the ideal distance also depends on the level of service you want. The closer you are to the exchange, the better the level of performance you will get. You can ask your ISP or Telco what the distance is or, if you're using a service such as ChunkyChips, you can use an online availability checker to see if you are close enough to receive service.

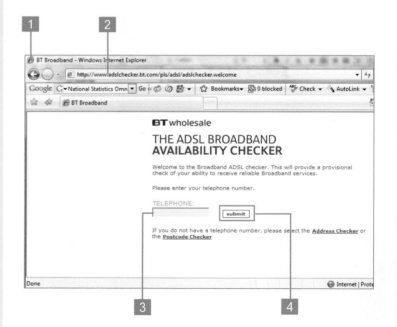

You can have a fast and reliable Internet connection, but if your broadband modem isn't functioning properly, you'd never know it. If your ISP tells you that the connection appears to be functioning correctly but you are still having service outages or slowdowns, it may be a good time to purchase a new broadband modem. What kind of modem should you get? That depends partly on the type of network you plan to install. Let's say that you plan to install a wireless network. Then you'll need a modem that has antennas and can transmit a wireless signal. But there are other factors, such as the type of modem, that can bring an improvement in performance as well.

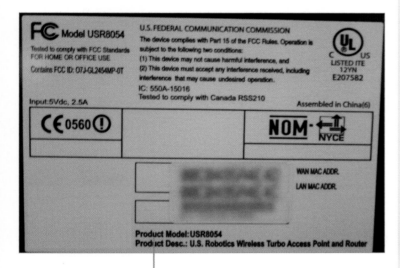

1

Getting a better broadband modem

1 Write down your current modem's model number and type so you have it when shopping for a new modem.

3

For your information

Your ISP is the place to start when you're looking for a broadband modem. It may offer to replace your hardware as part of your contract. Be sure to ask before you spend money on a new device. You've worked hard for your money, and there's no point in throwing it away for nothing.

Getting a better broadband modem (cont.)

2 Go to the Broadband Modems page on the UK Broadband Watchdog site at **http://www.broadbandwatchdog.co.uk/broadband-modems.php** and read about the difference between PCI and ADSL modems.

You can then go to sites that sell computer hardware, such as eBay UK (**http://www.ebay.co.uk**) or Amazon.co.uk (**http://www.amazon.co.uk**) to find one that suits your needs as well as your network.

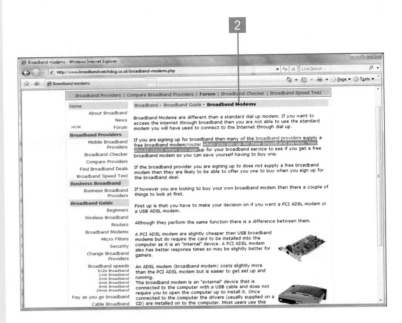

You might be perfectly satisfied with your Internet connection when you're the only person who uses it. When you enable other people in your home to share the same gateway, you might start to see your performance suffer. That's not to say you're going to have huge problems. In fact there are a few simple measures you can take to prevent trouble before it begins. Before you invite other users to download computer games or to watch video games online, it's a good idea to check your connection. Many online 'speed test' utilities are available; some compare your connection to others in your region so you know how your ISP stacks up. You might not need to switch providers if your connection is poor. A less drastic measure is to move up to a more robust package with your current ISP at a nominal extra cost.

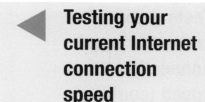

Testing your current Internet connection speed

1. Go to the Global Broadband Speed Test page (**http://www.speedtest.net/index.php**) and click the **triangle** representing the server nearest to your location. In the UK, for example, one server is located at Maidenhead.

2. Watch the speedometer move as the test is run, and evaluate the results when they appear.

3

1

2

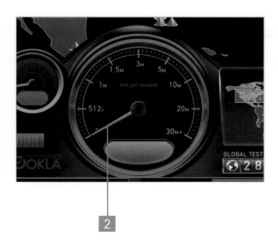

Testing your current Internet connection speed (cont.)

3 Click **My Results** to view more details about your connection, including latency.

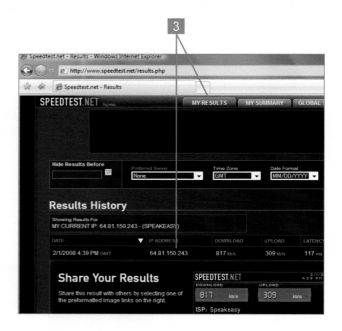

If your current connection is intermittent or not functioning, don't panic. I wouldn't recommend that you immediately switch to a different Internet Service Provider. In the first place, make sure the source of the problem isn't software that's malfunctioning or cables or other hardware that aren't working. Don't hesitate to call your ISP's technical support staff so they can guide you through the process. But if you prefer to do some work on your own, here are some quick tasks you can perform.

 ## Troubleshooting a broken connection

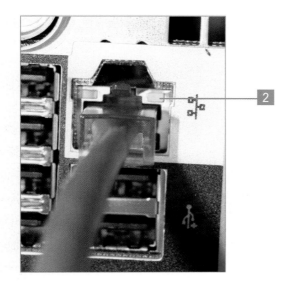

1 Sometimes a utility called Winsock that handles Internet connection tasks can be damaged. A utility called LSP-Fix is designed to repair it (**http://www.cexx.org/lspfix. htm**).

2 If you have an Ethernet connection to a single computer, make sure the cable is connected to that computer's Ethernet port (a blinking light should indicate that a connection is present).

3 Make sure the cable is securely plugged in to one of the ports on the router.

4 Scan your local network for viruses.

Configuring your Ethernet network

Introduction

Although wireless is continually growing in popularity, Ethernet is still a common networking method and is the perfect choice for networks that use desktop computers instead of laptops. Virtually all desktop computers these days are sold with Ethernet cards built in; the majority are not sold with built-in wireless capability. Therefore, if you have two, three, four or more desktop computers that you need to network, one of the best and easiest options is to connect them using Ethernet cable and a router. You won't regret the choice: Ethernet is a time-tested and reliable networking option that is easy to implement and widely supported. In fact, Windows XP and Vista both automatically configure Ethernet networks as soon as you 'plug in' your computer to get connected. This chapter explores tasks to get you started with your Ethernet network.

What you'll do

Let Windows automatically configure your network

Run Network Setup Wizard

Set up file and printer sharing

Directly connect two computers

Get connected to the Internet

Create a user account

Log on and off

Designate a network location

Set up Internet Connection Sharing

Locate your IP address information

Understand IP addresses, DNS servers and subnet masks

Letting Windows automatically configure your network

1. Power down your router by unplugging it.

2. Connect the broadband port on your router to your DSL or cable modem. (The broadband port is usually labelled WAN or Internet.)

3. Connect one end of an Ethernet cable to one of the ports on your hub.

4. If the computer you want to connect is running, click **Start** on the taskbar.

5. Click the arrow that points to the right.

6. Choose **Shut Down**.

Any shortcuts or timesaving steps with regard to creating a home network are welcome. Luckily for you, Windows Vista has the ability to automatically configure your network for you. Some of the subsequent tasks in this chapter discuss preliminary steps needed to establish an Ethernet network, such as purchasing cable and running the Network Setup Wizard.

But if you are in a hurry and you have your cable and router already installed and set up (perhaps with the help of a technically minded nephew, niece or grandchild), you can skip these tasks and take the 'express route'. In other words, let Windows automatically connect your computer to the Ethernet network. This task assume you have cable and router ready and just need to 'plug in'.

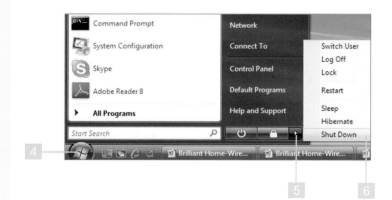

7. Connect one end of the Ethernet cable to one of the ports on your router. It doesn't matter which one, as long as you don't use the WAN or Internet port.

8. Connect the other end to the Ethernet port on your computer. Look for the Ethernet symbol above or next to the port. The symbol looks like a miniature network with three computers joined together.

9. Turn on your computer; Windows will automatically connect to the Internet. You'll know you're connected when you see the network connection symbol in the System Tray.

4

For your information

On Windows Vista, the icon has a blue symbol next to the two computer icons. On Windows Vista, the network connection is shown to be active when the two computers are both 'lit up' in blue.

Running Network Setup Wizard

One of the first tasks in configuring Ethernet in your home is to tell Windows Vista that you want to create a network in the first place. A system utility called Network Setup Wizard is designed to guide you through the process of creating the software foundation for your network. Once you have set up Windows to work with a network, you can start running the Ethernet cable and actually connecting hardware devices.

1 Click **Start** and choose **Control Panel**.

2 Double-click **Network Setup Wizard**. When the Welcome screen appears, click **Next**.

3 Click the button next to 'Turn on file and printer sharing'.

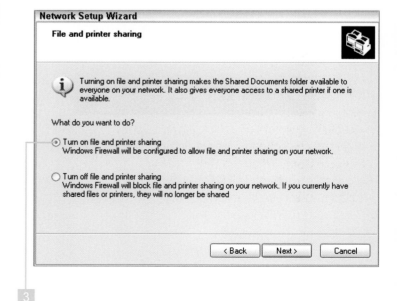

Network Setup Wizard

Select a connection method.

Select the statement that best describes this computer:

○ This computer connects directly to the Internet. The other computers on my network connect to the Internet through this computer.
View an example.

⊙ This computer connects to the Internet through a residential gateway or through another computer on my network.
View an example.

○ Other

Learn more about home or small office network configurations.

[< Back] [Next >] [Cancel]

4

4 Click the button next to 'This computer connects to the Internet through a residential gateway...' and then click **Next**.

5 Assign a short, easy-to-remember name to your computer and click **Next**.

6 Name your workgroup (see Chapter 1); click **Next**.

7 Click **Finish**.

8 Repeat the process on all of your other PCs, making sure to use the same workgroup name for all of them.

4

Did you know?

On Windows XP, the default workgroup name is MSHOME. You can change the name as part of the Network Setup Wizard, which is XP's tool for establishing a network. Click **Start**, **Control Panel** to open the control panel, and then double-click **Network Setup Wizard**. When the first screen of the wizard appears, click **Next**. Follow the steps in subsequent screens to set up your network and give it a name.

Setting up file and printer sharing

Once you have run Network Setup Wizard, you need to create a shared folder on your computer – a folder that contains the files you want to share on your home network. You need to set up a shared folder whether you have a client–server network or whether you have a peer-to-peer network. The shared folder can contain subfolders that keep your shared files organised. The primary difference is that, on a client–server network, the shared folder exists on the file server. On a peer-to-peer network, each computer has a shared folder that it allows other users to access. Another difference is the number of files you have to share and the range of people who can access them. In a client–server configuration, the file server is typically accessed by all of the computers on the network. In a peer-to-peer network, you may or may not share any files, and you may decide to share only with one person; the choice is up to the individual user.

1 Click **Start** and choose **Computer** from the Start menu.

If you are using Windows XP, click **Start** and choose **My Computer**.

2 Click the drive or folder in which the shared folder will be contained.

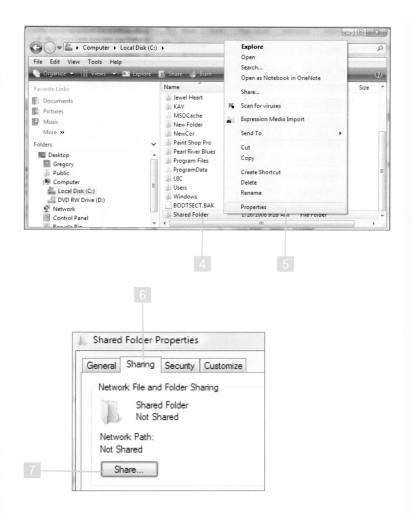

3 Click **File>New>Folder**.

4 Type a name for the new folder and press **Enter**.

5 Right-click the file name and choose **Properties**.
6 Click the **Sharing** tab.

7 Click **Share**.

8 Click a user name if the one you want is visible, or chose an option from the drop-down list.

9 Click **Share**.

4

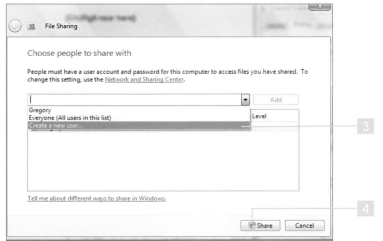

Directly connecting two computers

You don't need a router to connect two or more computers. By making use of a special type of Ethernet cable called a crossover cable, you can directly connect two computers and avoid the need for a router altogether. This kind of setup enables the two machines to share an Internet connection. There is a limitation, however: the machines have to be physically located close enough to one another for the cable to make the connection. If you buy a long cable or make your own, the machines can be located in different areas of your residence, however. Other types of cables such as a special USB cable or null modem serial cable can be used to connect one computer to another, but Ethernet gives you the best speed and reliability.

1. Buy a CAT-5 crossover cable at your local computer store. The cable should be clearly labelled as such.

2. Plug one end of the cable into one PC's Ethernet port. (This port will probably be part of the computer's Ethernet adapter.)

3. Plug the other end into the Ethernet card on the other PC.

4. If you want the two computers to share an Internet connection, you'll need to turn on Internet connection sharing on one of them, as described earlier in this chapter.

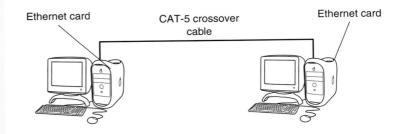

Ethernet card   CAT-5 crossover cable   Ethernet card

If the express network setup method described in this chapter's first task doesn't work, or if you feel you need to follow a more deliberate, step-by-step approach, you should begin in a systematic way. Most individuals who plan to set up a home network do so because they want to share a connection among two or more computers. If this is the reason why you're setting up a network, your first step is to either set up an Internet connection or make sure the one you currently have is functioning. Your Internet Service Provider or cable provider will help you get started by providing you with a modem and making sure the necessary lines are run to your house. After that, you'll need to follow some simple steps.

Connecting to the Internet

1. Using the cable that comes with the device, connect your broadband modem to the connector that brings the Internet connection to your house. You may only need a conventional phone cable for this purpose. (Make sure your broadband modem is off.)

2. Connect the broadband modem to the WAN or Internet port of the router.

4

For your information

If you have another Internet-based service such as Voice over Internet Protocol (VoIP), you might have another device between your broadband modem and your router. I have a second modem especially for VoIP, which is positioned between my DSL modem and my router. The VoIP modem has its own WAN or Internet port, which then connects to the WAN or Internet port on the router. The three devices – DSL modem, VoIP modem and router – all have to be turned on one after another.

Connecting to
the Internet
(cont.)

3 With an Ethernet cable, connect the Ethernet port on the broadband modem to the WAN or Internet port on your router.

4 Turn on your broadband modem and wait until the DSL or cable light stops blinking and stays on constantly.

5 Turn on your router and wait until the Internet or WAN light stops blinking and stays on constantly.

Did you know?

If your DSL or cable modem does not display a solid DSL or cable light, and the light won't stop blinking, call your ISP to troubleshoot the connection. The problem may be with the junction box outside your house that brings your DSL or cable service inside.

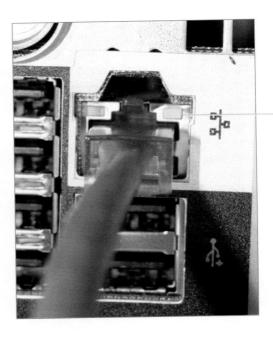

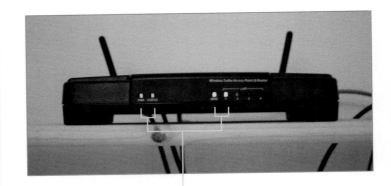

If you are the only person who uses your computer and you don't plan to network with other computers at home or in the office, a user account isn't essential. Having said that, however, it's always a good idea to protect your computer from unauthorised access with a username and a password. That way, if your computer is lost or stolen, a criminal will find it difficult if not impossible to get at your critical information. But if you're on a network with other users, a user account is critical. Don't leave your default account name (for instance, Administrator) in place; protect yourself with a unique and hard-to-guess account name and a password that will be difficult for hackers to 'crack'.

◀ **Creating a user account**

1 Click the **Start** button on the taskbar.

2 Choose **Control Panel**.

3 Click **Add or remove user accounts**.

4 Click **Create a new account**.

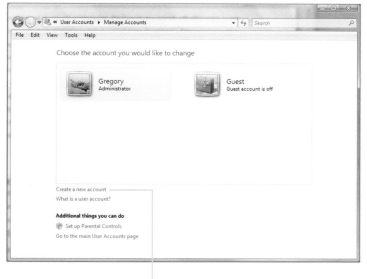

Creating a user account (cont.)

5. Type a name for the account.

6. Leave **Standard user** selected.

7. Click **Create Account**.

8. Click the name of the account you just created.

9. Click **Create a password**.

For your information

The Guest account is created by default and, by default, it is turned off. Leave this account turned off and don't use it to give others in your household access to your computer. The Guest account can be a security risk. Instead, create a separate account with a unique password and username.

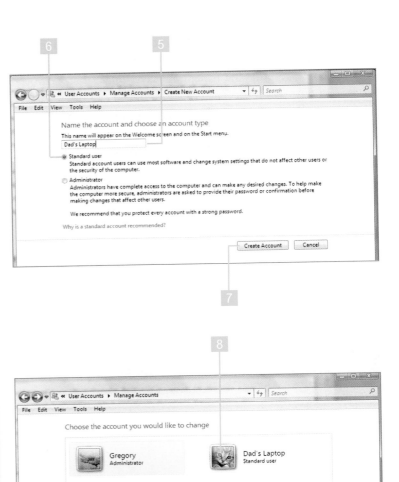

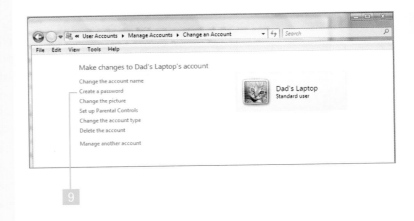

Once you are part of a network, you need to get in the habit of logging on to the network with your username and password when you start working. That way, you can gain access to any folders and files that are associated with your account. For instance, if a shared folder called Finances has been set up and given access to the users Tom, Dick and Harry, you have to log in with one of those usernames to access it – not a different user account you might have, such as Administrator. Logging on and off is a simple matter and will quickly become second nature to you.

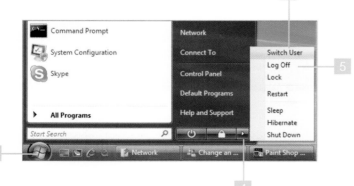

Logging on and off

1 Once you have a user account established, you'll be prompted for it when you log on. Click the icon that appears when Windows finishes booting up; your username should appear beneath it.

2 Enter your password when prompted and press **Log On**.

3 When you need to log off, click the **Start** button on the taskbar.

4 Click the arrow that points to the right.

5 Choose **Log Off** from the context menu. You'll be prompted to save any files that have unsaved information before you log off.

6 If you have more than one account and need to switch from one to another, choose **Switch User**.

See also

See the preceding task for instructions on how to set up a user account.

Designating a network location

Once you have the network hardware you need and have a connection established to the Internet, you can start connecting other computers to your network. First, choose a location for your network. You have three options:

- **Home**. You designate the network as being part of your home or your small home-based business: all of the computers are known and trusted.

- **Work**. Although Work and Home are two different designations, the level of security is the same: the computers are treated by the firewall as ones you trust.

- **Public**. This designation has a higher level of security than Home or Work. Windows won't automatically detect other computers on the same network as you, for instance. In a public place such as a coffee shop or airport, you can't trust the computer users around you.

1. Log on to your network using the username and password that you have associated with it. (You may need to choose **Log Off** if you are currently logged on with another account.)

2. Click **Start** and choose **Network**.

3. Choose **Network and Sharing Center**.

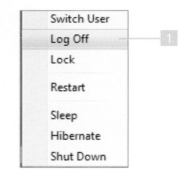

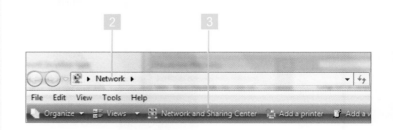

Why is it important to select a network location? For one thing, it controls the level of security imposed by the built-in firewall program that comes as part of Windows. You need to make sure your network is designated as Home or Work so Windows can perform network discovery. Network discovery detects other computers attached to your network.

4 Click **Customize**.

5 Change the name of the network if you wish.

6 Choose **Public** or **Private** to change the type of network.

7 Click **Change** and choose a new icon if you wish.

8 Click **Next**.

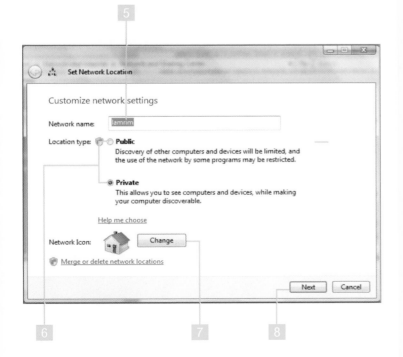

Designating a network location (cont.)

9 Click **View or change network and sharing settings...** if you need to change settings further.

10 If the settings are acceptable, click **Close**.

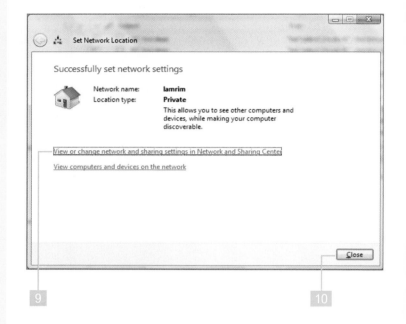

9   10

Even if you're only connecting two computers in a simple ad-hoc network, you can still share an Internet connection between them. To do that you'll need to set up Internet Connection Sharing (ICS). ICS enables you to share a connection with other computers that are connected to yours. Once you have your Internet connection up and running and your router configured, connect one computer to the router as described in 'Letting Windows automatically configure your network'. Then follow these steps.

Setting up Internet Connection Sharing

1. Click the **Start** button on the taskbar.
2. Choose **Control Panel**.
3. Click **View network status and tasks**.
4. Click **Manage network connections**.

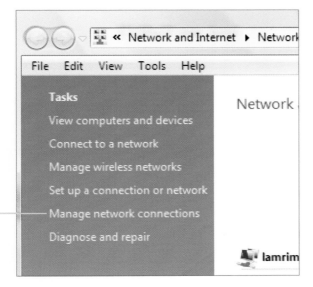

Setting up Internet Connection Sharing (cont.)

5 Right-click the connection you want to share and choose **Properties** from the context menu.

6 If a User Account Control dialogue box appears, click **Continue**.

7 Click the **Sharing** tab.

8 Click the box next to 'Allow other network users to connect through this computer's Internet connection'.

9 Click **OK**.

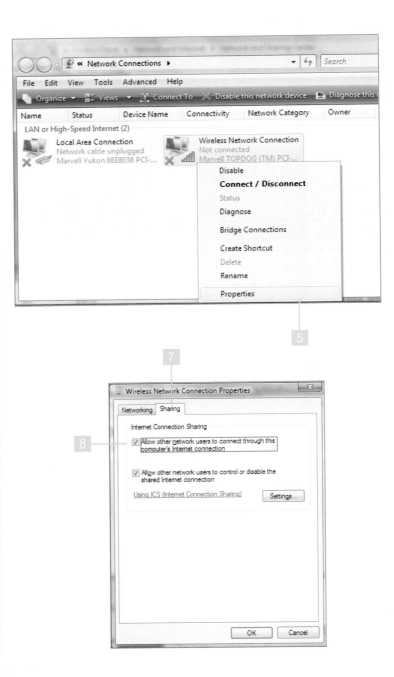

Every computer that is connected to the Internet is assigned an Internet Protocol (IP) address – a unique number that distinguishes it from other networked computers and that enables information to reach it. IP addresses fall into two general categories:

- **Dynamic**. The address is dynamically assigned each time you connect to the network; it can change from one session to another.

- **Static**. You are assigned a single, non-changing address by your Internet Service Provider; you have the same address every time you connect to the network.

Depending on the kind of Internet access account you have, when you first sign up for an Internet access account with an ISP, your provider will give you the IP addresses of its domain name servers. These DNS addresses are essential. DNS servers translate URLs with domain names like **http://www.pearson.com** into IP addresses. You need to enter them so your computer can connect to websites.

Locating your IP address information

1 Follow steps 1–5 from the preceding task.

2 Click **Internet Protocol Version 6** or **Internet Protocol Version 4**. (If you don't know what version you are using, ask your ISP.)

3 Click **Properties**.

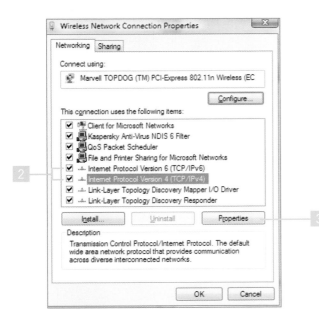

Locating your IP address information (cont.)

4 Click **Use the following DNS server addresses**.

5 Enter the addresses in the spaces provided. (Press the right arrow key to move from one section to another.)

6 Click **OK**.

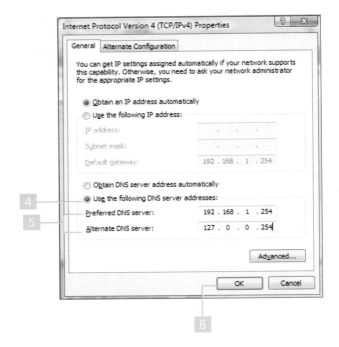

Understanding IP addresses, DNS servers and subnet masks

To view the basic details about your current connection, click **Start** and choose **Network**, and then click **Network and Sharing Center**. Right-click the name of the network connection you are currently using and choose **Properties**. When the status dialogue box appears for your connection, click **Details**.

■ **DNS:** Domain Name Service is a system that uses recognisable aliases like speakeasy.net or pearson.com in place of hard-to-remember IP addresses.

■ **Physical address:** The Media Access Control (MAC) address of your network adapter. Adapters use MAC addresses to uniquely identify themselves on the network.

■ **DHCP:** Dynamic Host Control Protocol, a protocol that enables IP addresses to be

assigned dynamically to computers on a network.

■ **IP address:** Internet Protocol address, a series of numbers or characters that uniquely identifies a computer on the Internet. IPv4 numbers consist of four sets of numbers separated by dots. IPv6 numbers are longer and more complex.

■ **Private IP address:** Some IP addresses are reserved for use on internal networks and cannot be accessed directly from the Internet. Chances are you use dynamically assigned, private IP addresses on your network.

■ **DNS server:** A computer provided by your ISP that enables you to access websites by translating their domain names into IP addresses.

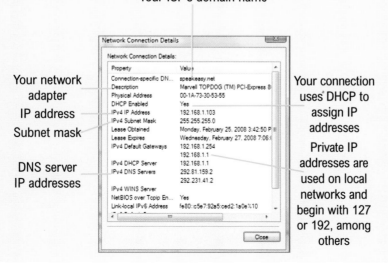

Your ISP's domain name

Your network adapter
IP address
Subnet mask

DNS server
IP addresses

Your connection uses DHCP to assign IP addresses

Private IP addresses are used on local networks and begin with 127 or 192, among others

Installing and configuring your Ethernet network

5

Introduction

When you make the decision to create an Ethernet-based network, you have to face the inescapable fact that you'll need to work with cable. You don't need to be an electrician, and you don't need to be an expert in home repair. You do, however, need to familiarise yourself with the basics about Ethernet cable and when to use specialised varieties of cable for specific tasks. This chapter will teach you the basics about running cable and how to make the best use of it in your house.

What you'll do

Build your own Ethernet cable

Run your networking cables

Review special types of Ethernet cables

Extend an Ethernet cable

Understand unshielded twisted pair (UTP) cable

Understand Power-over-Ethernet (PoE)

Bridge two long-range Ethernet devices

Merge network locations

Adjust your IP address information

Connect another computer to your network and workgroup

Building your own Ethernet cable

1. An RJ-45 crimp tool.
2. A box of RJ-45 connectors.
3. A box of CAT-5 cable.
4. Pull out the desired length of cable from the box you purchased and cut it with your crimping tool.

Ethernet cable can be expensive if you buy it in long length – and often, you need many metres' worth of cable to stretch from one part of your home to another. A 20 m length of cable might cost £6.49. But if you build the same length of cable yourself, you can reduce the cost even more. If you only need a single cable, you might not want to go to the trouble of creating your own. But if you expect to create three, four or five cables, it can be worth the investment. You will also need some tools.

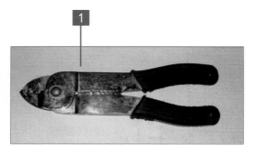

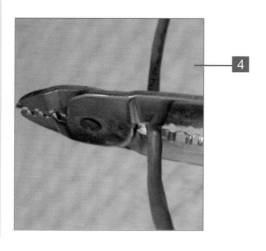

Building your own Ethernet cable (cont.)

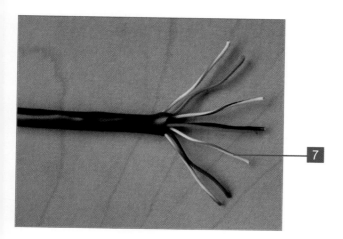

5 Use the wire stripper to strip about one inch of the outer sheath from the cable.

6 Take care to cut only the outer sheath and leave the coverings on the individual wires. You should see four pairs of twisted wires protruding from the outer sheath. (This is where the name twisted-pair cabling comes from.)

7 Separate the four pairs of wires and untwist them so you have eight wires.

5

Building your own Ethernet cable (cont.)

8 Arrange the wires this way for a straight (or straight through) cable (a cable that connects a computer to a hub).

9 Arrange the wires this way for a crossover cable.

10 Trim the wires so only about half an inch protrudes from the outer sheath.

11 Insert the wires in the RJ-45 connector. Make sure each wire fits in its chamber.

12 Place the RJ-45 jack in the crimp tool and crimp it, pressing down as hard as possible.

For your information

A straight or T-568A or T-568-B cable is used to connect a computer or other device to a router or hub. A crossover cable is used to connect one computer to another.

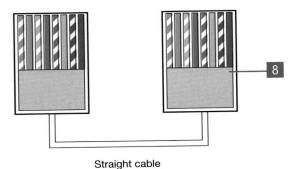

Straight cable

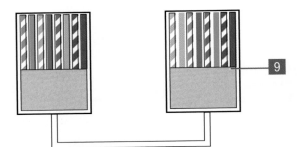

Crossover cable

Once you are able to make your own Ethernet cables, you can make them as long as you need to run from one room to another in your house. The question is this: where do you run the cables? How do you conceal the cables so they aren't easily seen? In general, you want to avoid having to drill holes in your walls and floor that will be unsightly. It's preferable to use existing furnishings and features to hide your cable. Here are a few tips.

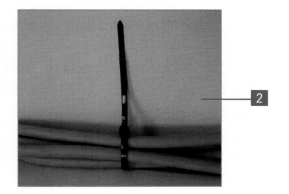

1 Lift up the edge of your carpeting and run your cable under it, taking care not to pierce the cable on any nails or carpet-grabbers underneath.

2 Run your cable through existing holes alongside other wires. Use twist ties to keep your cable from getting tangled.

5

Did you know?

When you run cable, always leave a metre or two of slack in case you need to reposition devices. Keep the cable at least a metre away from fluorescent lights and other sources of electrical interference. Be sure to cover the cable if you run it across a floor, so people don't trip on it.

Understanding Ethernet cable: an either/or decision

All Ethernet cable is not made alike. In fact, you need to take care when you purchase ready-made cable in the computer store. Do you need a null cable, a crossover cable, a CAT-5 or a serial cable? Do you know the differences between them? Each type of cable has a specific purpose and can carry a maximum amount of data.

The two general types

There are many varieties of Ethernet cable, but they fall into two general categories.

Straight-through cable (also called CAT-5 cable) connects a router or hub with a computer, printer or other device.

Crossover cable (also called CAT-5 crossover cable) connects two computers directly so they can share files. However, some cable television providers require crossover cable to connect devices to the cable modem. If you see a socket marked X-over on the back of the modem, this indicates that a crossover cable is required.

Structure and speed

Within either of the two general types, you have ways of constructing the cable so that it can transmit a particular amount of digital information.

The choice of cable depends on the type of Ethernet card you have installed. Of these, the 10Base-T, which can transmit up to 10 Mbps, and 100Base-T, which can transmit up to 100 Mbps, are the most common.

Cable length	Construction	Maximum
10Base-T	Unshielded twisted pair	100 metres
100Base-T	Unshielded twisted pair	100 metres
10Base-2	Thin coaxial cable	180 metres
10Base-5	Thick coaxial cable	500 metres
10Base-F	Fibre optic cable	2000 metres
100Base-TX	Unshielded twisted pair	220 metres

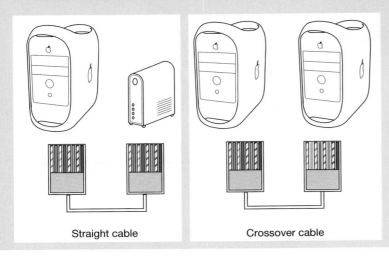

Straight cable   Crossover cable

Suppose you have a situation where you need an Internet connection to stretch a long distance – say, from your main house to another building on your property such as a garage – and you want to use Ethernet. But conventional 10Base-T or 100Base-T cable only reaches 100 metres. If that's the case, you have a couple of options available for extending the cable.

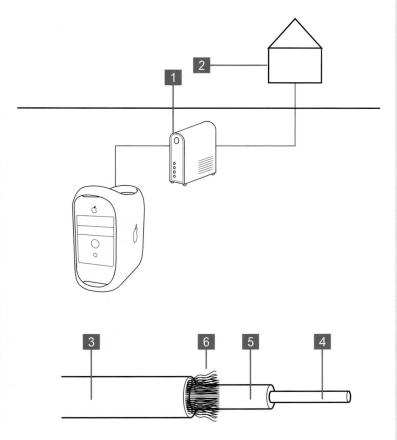

Extending Ethernet cable

Option 1: Add a switch or hub

1 Purchase an inexpensive switch or hub and plug one end of one cable into it.

2 Plug a second cable into another port on the switch or hub and extend it to the computer in the other building.

Option 2: Switch to fibre optic

3 Switch from unshielded twisted pair cable to fibre optic. It's more expensive but can reach up to 2000 metres. The outer jacket insulates the cable.

4 The fibre optic centre is made of glass or plastic and must be protected

5 A plastic coating covers the fibre centre.

6 Kevlar fibres prevent breakage.

5

Understanding unshielded twisted pair (UTP) cable

The most common type of cable used with LANs is unshielded twisted pair. This is the type of wiring used in 10Base-T or 100Base-T cable. It's also an inexpensive type of Ethernet cable that performs well because of the way it's constructed. The twisted pairs of wires that make up the cable insulate it from interference from other electrical devices.

The Electronic Industry Association/ Telecommunication Industry Association (EIA/TIA) has created five categories of unshielded twisted pair cable.

1 The cable is made up of twisted pairs.

2 The twisted pairs are contained within an outer jacket.

- Category 1: Voice Only (used for telephone)

- Category 2: Local Talk data transmission up to 4 Mbps

- Category 3: Ethernet data transmission up to 10 Mbps

- Category 4: Token Ring data transmission up to 20 Mbps

- Category 5: Fast Ethernet data transmission up to 100 Mbps.

The cost goes up from one category to the next, with Category 5 being the most expensive. But, if you can afford Category 5, it will give you the highest level of quality. Shielded twisted pair cable has a metal shielding around the twisted pairs but is susceptible to radio and electronic interference, and the shielding makes the cable quite bulky.

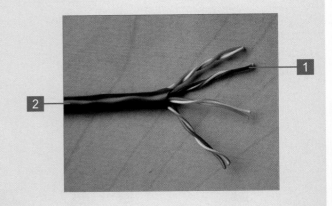

Understanding Power-over-Ethernet (PoE)

Digital information of the sort exchanged by computers isn't the only thing you can get over Ethernet cable. Electrical power can also be distributed over Ethernet. It's a useful way to deliver power to devices that use IP technology, such as Voice over IP (VoIP) telephones and surveillance cameras. PoE has been approved as an international standard, IEEE802.3af, and is the first international standard for distributing electrical power.

Usually, a device such as a telephone or router requires that the device not only has a data connection but a separate power supply through an adapter plugged into one of your home's electrical sockets.

The usual CAT-5 Ethernet cable contains four twisted pairs, but only two are used for data communications. The others can be used for power. You can do this by adding a device called a power injector. This supplies (or 'injects') 48V DC into the Ethernet cables.

The power injector needs to plug into your home's existing power at an electrical outlet. PoE, in other words, doesn't alleviate the need to have electrical power, but it does save power because the injector and another device called a splitter distribute the power to multiple devices, such as network hubs, PCs and VoIP phones, as shown below.

You can purchase such injectors, as well as other PoE kits, at the Solwise website (**http://www.solwise.co.uk/ networking-copper-based-poe.htm**).

5

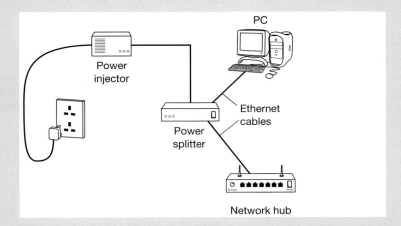

Bridging two long-range Ethernet devices

Suppose you have an Ethernet-based computer network at home and a second one at your small business in town several miles away. Is it possible to connect or 'bridge' the two networks in order to share files as well as Internet access between all of the computers in both locations? You can install a long-range wireless bridge, a device that uses wireless technology to connect two far-flung Ethernet networks. The long-range MaxStream Xpress Ethernet Bridge can make wireless connections of up to 15 miles – as long as the two points have an unobscured line of sight. The XPress Ethernet Bridge uses the seldom-used 900 Mhz frequency, so it won't interfere with 2.4 GHz or other wireless networks. It also encrypts and decrypts data sent across the bridge for greater security.

1. Go to the MaxStream website (**http://www.microdaq.com/maxstream/xpress/indoor.php**) and read about the Xpress Ethernet Bridge.

2. Choose the indoor or outdoor version of the Xpress Ethernet Bridge.

3. After you purchase the bridge package and it arrives, hook up one power adapter, one radio unit and one omni-directional antenna in each of the two locations you want to bridge.

4. Adjust the power adapter; it works with 80–240 volts AC so will work in the UK.

5. Adjust the DIP switches on the back of the unit as needed to find an appropriate wireless channel. If your network uses a switch or hub instead of a router, make sure DIP switch 1 is switched to ON.

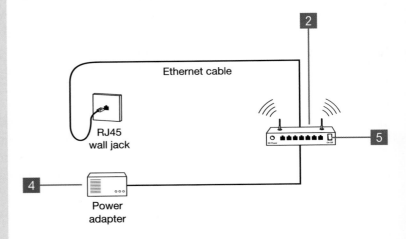

For your information

If you need to connect your laptop to your local network via Ethernet and you want to move around the house, purchase the retractable Ethernet cable from *The Independent* (**http://www.independentoffers.co.uk/I-GG-TEC4-EI-0/TEC4-Ethernet-CAT5-cable.htm**). The cable is contained within a hard plastic container; you only need to unroll the specific length you need, and the cable retracts when you're done for maximum portability.

In some special situations, you can end up with two network locations for the same connection. For instance, if your router permits both Ethernet and wireless access to the same home network, and you switch between one connection method and the other, you can have a home and public location designated for the same network. The problem is that if your network is intended to be private and one of the locations is designated as public, you have a security risk. You can easily solve the problem by merging the network locations.

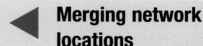

Merging network locations

1 Click **Start** and choose **Network**.

2 Click **Network and Sharing Center**.

3 Click **Customize** next to one of the connections you need to merge.

5

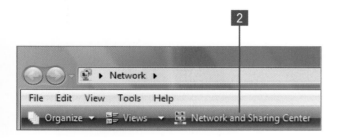

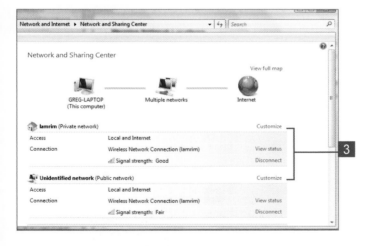

Merging network locations (cont.)

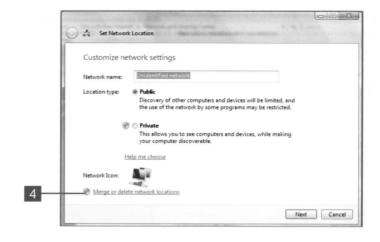

4 Click **Merge or delete network locations**.

5 If a User Account Control dialogue box appears, click **Continue**.

6 Click any networks you no longer use and click **Delete** to remove each one from the list.

7 Click the network you want to merge and click **Merge**.

8 Click the network into which you want to merge the previously selected network.

9 Click **OK**.

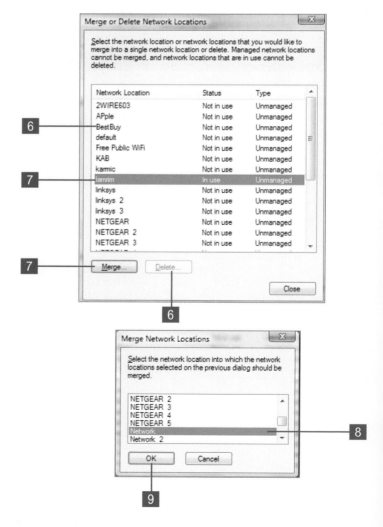

Every computer that is connected to the Internet is assigned an Internet Protocol (IP) address – a unique number that distinguishes it from other networked computers and that enables information to reach it. IP addresses fall into two general categories:

- **Dynamic**. The address is dynamically assigned each time you connect to the network; it can change from one session to another.

- **Static**. You are assigned a single, non-changing address by your Internet Service Provider; you have the same address every time you connect to the network.

Depending on the kind of Internet access account you have, when you first sign up for an Internet access account with an ISP, your provider will give you the IP addresses of its domain name servers. These DNS addresses are essential. DNS servers translate URLs with domain names like **http://www.pearson.com** into IP addresses. You need to enter them so your computer can connect to websites.

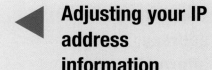

Adjusting your IP address information

1 Follow steps 1–5 from the preceding task.

2 Click **Internet Protocol Version 6 or Internet Protocol Version 4**. (If you don't know what version you are using, ask your ISP.)

3 Click **Properties**.

5

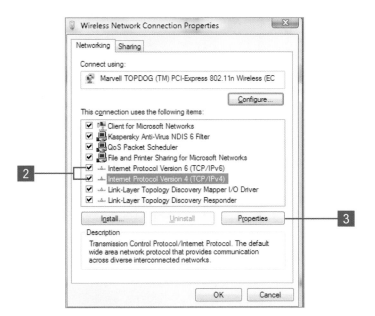

Did you know?

Chances are your Internet access account will enable you to connect only with a dynamic IP address. You have to pay your ISP extra for an account that uses static addresses because they are in short supply; they are primarily useful if you intend to run a web server.

Adjusting your IP address information (cont.)

4 Click **Use the following DNS server addresses**.

5 Enter the addresses in the spaces provided. (Press the right arrow key to move from one section to another.)

6 Click **OK**.

Once you have connected two or more computers to the Internet and to one another using a router, hub, switch or other conventional network device, it's relatively easy to add another computer to the network.

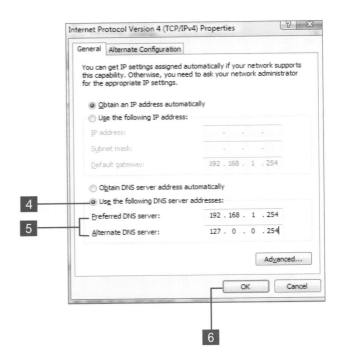

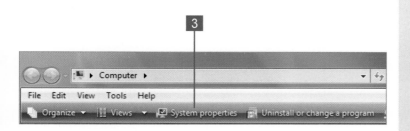

Verify your workgroup name

1 Click the **Start** button on the taskbar.

2 Choose **Computer**.

3 Click **System properties**.

4 Write down the name of your workgroup exactly as it appears.

5 Switch to the computer you want to add, follow steps 1–4, and click **Change settings**.

5

Connecting
another computer
to your network
and workgroup
(cont.)

6 Click **Change**.

7 Enter the name of the PC

8 Enter the workgroup name.

9 Click **OK**.

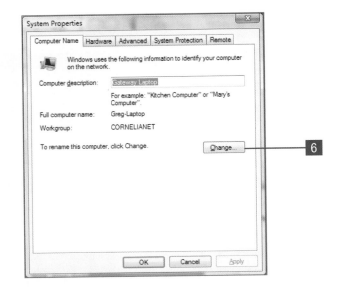

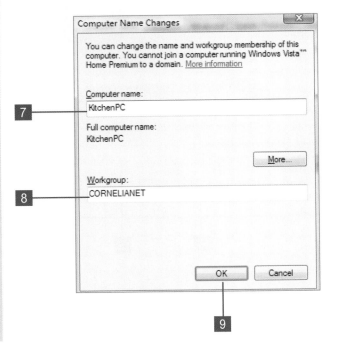

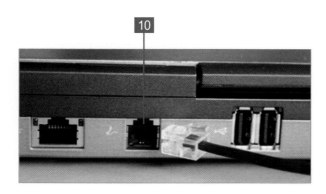

10

10 Plug one end of an Ethernet cable into the Ethernet card or port of the computer you want to add to your network, and the other end into a router.

11 Click **Start** and choose **Network**.

12 Double-click the down arrow next to **Workgroup** and choose your workgroup from the list presented.

13 Verify that your computer and others on your network are presented in the list of networked computers.

5

11 **12**

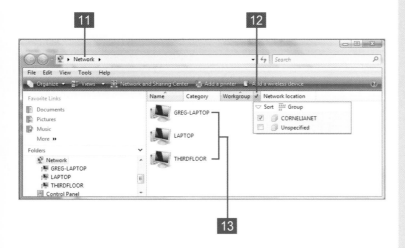

13

Using existing wiring

Introduction

If you're reading this book, you've probably already decided that you want to connect your computers together so they can share files and use the same Internet connection. But now you have another decision to make: how are you going to set up those lines of communication between your computers?

You've got two basic options: wired or wireless. For many people (especially those who are just getting started with computers and the Internet), a computer network created with 'solid' wiring rather than wireless signals seems more reliable and yields a better connection than one that uses wireless technology. Yet, the prospect of buying wiring and stringing Ethernet cable through floors or walls, or along carpeting, is too much of a hassle. It's only natural to ask: wouldn't it be great if the wiring needed to connect computers is already available within the walls of your home? In fact, in some new construction projects, Ethernet cabling is provided inside the walls, ready to plug in and use.

However, even if you don't have Ethernet cabling available, you already have two other feasible kinds of wiring already present: your existing electrical mains and phone lines. You can piggyback on to your home's electrical cables and sockets to create computer networks through a technology referred to as a home power, Powerline or HomePlug network. (This chapter will primarily use the generic term 'home power'.) Or you can do the same with your phone lines. All you need is some inexpensive hardware and some know-how, and you'll be streaming music and surfing the Web throughout your home with more no additional wiring than you already have.

What you'll do

Buy and install a network extender kit

Set up a HomePlug network

Build a bridge to your broadband connection

Configure a HomePNA phone wiring network

Understand the pros and cons of structured wiring

Buying and installing a network extender kit

One type of network connection that uses your home's electrical wiring is a *network extender*. An extender is not a tool for creating a complete home network, but rather hardware that extends a wireless or Ethernet network into rooms where it wouldn't reach otherwise. (You'll learn more about wireless networks in the next chapter of this book.) In this task, you'll learn how to use your home wiring connection to improve wireless network performance.

1 Connect the network extender component of the kit to your router with an Ethernet cable.

2 Plug the connector into one of your home's electrical outlets.

3 Connect the network adapter component to the device you want to network with a separate cable.

4 Plug the second connector into an outlet, making sure that it is on the same circuit as the other connector.

5 Wait for your computer to connect to the network. Check the network connection in the System Tray to make sure the computer is connected.

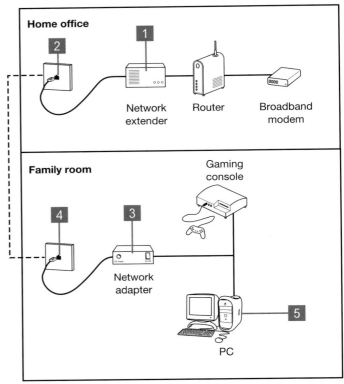

For your information

You could purchase the Powerline Ethernet Adapter kit directly from Netgear and a single Powerline Wireless-G Range Extender. They need to be running Windows 98 or later to enable them to encrypt your data. Both the Ethernet and wireless version of the adapter kits can be found at: **http://www.netgear.com/Products/Powerline Networking/PowerlineEthernetAdapters.aspx**.

There are several advantages to using your home's existing electrical wiring to connect your computers, especially since the digital information that flows to and from your computers doesn't interfere with your power mains.

Many people choose home power networking as a way of extending an existing Ethernet or Wi-Fi network. But home power hardware can also be used to create a complete home network. As long as you purchase the right hardware, you should have your network up and running in no time at all.

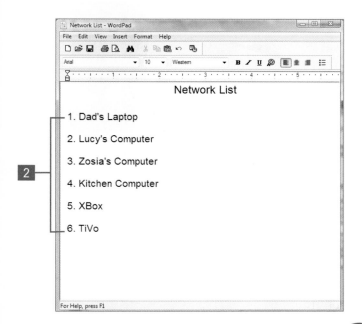

Setting up a HomePlug network

6

Assess your needs

1. Make a list of any hard-to-reach spots in your home.

2. Make a list of all the networked devices you plan to add. The networking standard that makes home owner networks possible has a built-in limit of 16 devices at any one time. If you need more, switch to Ethernet.

For your information

By now you've probably learned that nothing is perfect, and there are reasons that home power isn't as popular as Ethernet or Wi-Fi for networking. Keep in mind that home power isn't as fast as Ethernet. The fast Ethernet option that's widely in use transmits data at 100 Mbps, while home power has a maximum speed of 14 Mbps and a typical speed of 5–8 Mbps. And if your electrical system at home isn't adequate for your appliances and other needs, your Internet connection can slow even further. Home power equipment can also be pricey.

Setting up a HomePlug network (cont.)

Choose the right hardware

1. You will need a router, at least one network adapter, and some short-range Ethernet cables.

2. Make sure the hardware is approved by the HomePlug Powerline Alliance. (**http://www.homeplug.org**).

3. Make sure 56-bit encryption is provided so that your data will be secure.

4. Make sure the device will continue to transmit data even if the power line performance fluctuates.

5. Make sure the device supports UK, not US, wiring.

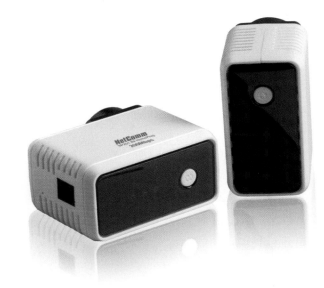

See also

The tasks in this chapter focus primarily on using HomePlug or Powerline hardware combined with Ethernet cables to create a home network. However, as mentioned above you can easily use home power networking hardware to create a hybrid network that reaches all parts of your house.

You may have already faced the challenge of extending the TV signal throughout your house when you first got cable service. Now you're facing the same situation with your Internet connection. Suppose you just obtained a new DSL or cable modem service. You want to network two or more devices, and you want them to share Internet access. You can 'bridge' your connection by installing a home power router or switch. Just follow the steps below.

1. Plug your Powerline router or switch into the wall
2. Plug one end of an Ethernet cable into your cable or DSL modem.
3. Plug the other end into the Powerline router or switch.
4. Plug network adapters as needed into wall outlets and connect them to the devices you need to network.

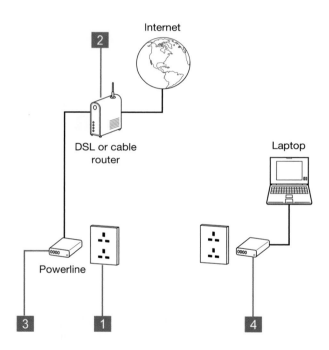

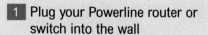

Did you know?

Broadbandbuyer.co.uk offers a Dynamode R-ADSL-C4-2 ADSL router. It has a built-in firewall as well as four ports for 10/00 Ethernet cables. This means you can use the device with home power or Ethernet

Configuring a HomePNA phone wiring network

1 Purchase an adapter. The adapter connects your computer or other device to the phone system in your house. Adapters are available in the form of a USB device or a card you install in your PC or laptop.

2 Plug one end of a cable into the network adapter on your computer.

3 Plug the other end of the cable into one of your telephone wall jacks.

4 If you need Internet access, plug one end of a phone cable into your router or hub. Plug one end into a phone jack.

There is yet another option available to you. Phoneline networks also use lines that are already in your house to send and receive digital information. In contrast to Powerline devices, which make use of your power mains, Phoneline uses existing phone cables to connect computers. The idea is that, since plain old telephone service telephones don't use all frequencies that are needed by a typical phone cable, the extra lines can be used by computers to exchange data.

Phoneline technology usually goes by the name of its standard, HomePNA. The standard has been through three versions. You should look for network adapters and other components that conform to HomePNA Version 3.0, which allows for data transfer rates of up to 128 Mbps. (The earlier two versions, 1.0 and 2.0, provide for transfer rates of 1 Mbps and 10 Mbps, respectively.) So here's what you need to do if you decide to go this route (no pun intended).

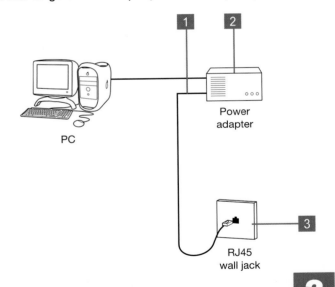

PC

Power adapter

RJ45 wall jack

Did you know?

ComputerActive offers a BT Wireless Router that also supports the HomePNA 2.0 standard so you can create a wireless network and extend it with HomePNA adapters. The router sells for £179 and the adapter for £39.99. Go to **http://www.computeractive.co.uk/ personal-computer-world/hardware/2044791/ bt-wireless-network-1250** to find out more.

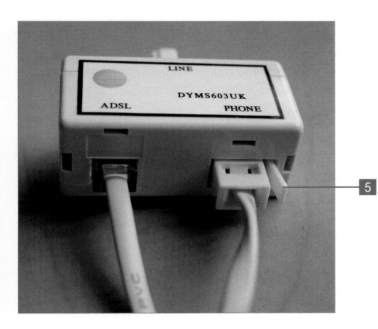

5

Combining a phone and a computer

5 If you need a telephone to use the same phone jack as your computer, purchase a splitter. A splitter divides a single phone jack into two. Plug the splitter into your phone jack, and use the two jacks on the splitter for your computer and your phone.

For your information

You've probably asked someone: 'Are we on the same page?' Now you need to ask: 'Are we on the same line?' Make sure all of the phone jacks you use to connect the computers in your house are on the same phone line. If you have more than one phone number in your house, make sure all the network devices are on a single line.

Note: If you have had the phones disconnected for some reason but the lines and jacks are still available, you can use them for networking. A dial tone is not necessary for this purpose.

Pros and cons of structured wiring

Is Powerline or Phoneline for you? Here are some pros and cons to consider if you're still scratching your head and wondering about the best way to get your computers to 'talk' to one another.

Keep in mind that the term 'structured wiring' is occasionally used to describe wiring that is part of an existing structure, as opposed to wiring you install (for instance, Ethernet cable). Using structured wiring for a computer network has the obvious advantage of convenience: the wire is already in place, so you don't have to install it. You might well ask, then, why structured wiring isn't more popular, and why most of the networking hardware you see in the local electronics store is intended for Ethernet or Wi-Fi networks. The advantages and disadvantages of structured wiring are as follows.

Advantages

- Structured wiring can be used to extend a wireless or Ethernet network.
- Nearly all home devices have encryption and surge suppression built in.
- Setup is complete in a matter of minutes.
- Structured wiring can give you better speed performance than wireless.

Disadvantages

- Most phone and home power network wiring is not as fast as Ethernet.
- You do occasionally run into connection problems.
- Adapters and other components are pricey.

Learning about Wi-Fi networks

Introduction

If you're just getting up to speed with computers and the Internet, words like Wi-Fi are probably confusing: they might even seem intimidating. In this book, I'll try to be as user-friendly as possible by providing translations in plain English. Instead of using the term 'Wi-Fi', for example, I'll say 'wireless'. It simply means that, like radio, information is sent from a transmitter to a receiver through the air, without a wire. In this case, the signal contains digital information of the sort your computer can use. The transmitter is a wireless router you install in your house; the 'receiver' is a device such as a wireless card installed in your laptop or desktop computer.

Wireless networks are chosen by most users these days. The obvious advantage of using wireless technology is freedom: you don't need to run cables through the walls or floors. If you have a wireless card in your laptop, you can pick up and move your computer anywhere in your house. Another good selling point is ease of use: it's easy to get the system up and running without the labour of stringing cables.

Of course, wireless signals don't always work perfectly the first time in every situation. Brick walls, pipes and other structural features can leave you connecting and reconnecting in frustration. Luckily, you know from Chapter 6 how to extend your network with phoneline or home power adapters. This chapter will describe what you need to know and how to plan out your wireless network so you can install it successfully.

What you'll do

Map out your networking needs

Project the number of computers you want to network and their location

Decide where you're going to use Wi-Fi

Position your router and network devices

Understand Wi-Fi protocols

Understand what a MAC address is and why you need to know about it

Know about the features you'll find in wireless access points

Mapping out your networking needs

If you're shopping for a dining room set, you need to think about how many chairs and settings you need. Likewise, some advance planning will come in handy further down the road when you choose the hardware for a wireless network. Knowing what you need will help you make smart purchases the first time so you can avoid reconfiguring the network or purchasing additional equipment later on.

Take a site survey

1. Write down the names of the people in your household who will use the network.

2. Ask them what they want to do on the Internet or local network, and what applications they want to use.

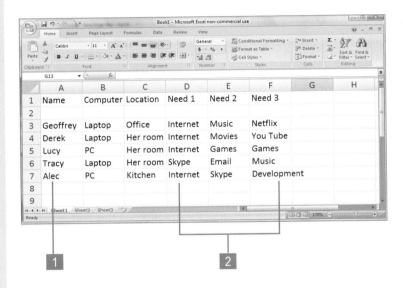

Did you know?

802.11a has a maximum data rate of 11 Mbps; 802.11g can reach a data rate of 54 Mbps. The newer 802.11n standard has a top speed of 100 Mbps.

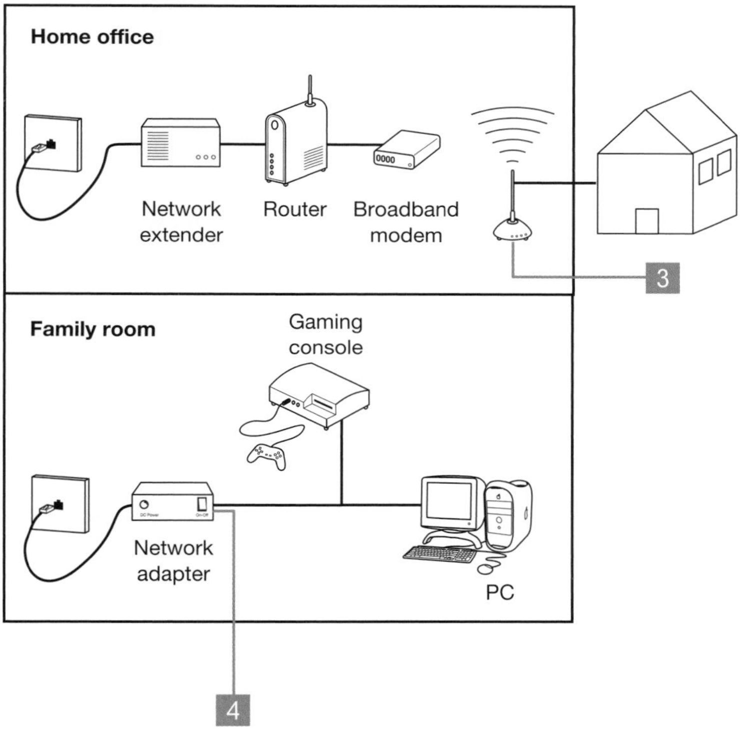

Mapping out your networking needs (cont.)

Home office

Network extender · Router · Broadband modem

3

Family room

Gaming console

Network adapter

PC

4

Take a needs survey

3 If one of the goals of your network is to provide Internet access to an outlying building, measure the distance to the building. Buy a wireless router that will transmit over the distance needed, or plan to buy an extra antenna.

4 If you need maximum data transmission speeds because people using your network will download movies, play games or perform other bandwidth intensive functions, make sure you choose hardware that supports a faster protocol.

7

Projecting the number of computers you want to network and their location

1. Decide which of your computers you want to network.

2. Decide whether the computers to be networked will be all one OS or mixed (Macs, PCs, Linux).

3. Decide how many devices you will have on the wireless part of your network, and how many will use Ethernet, home power or phoneline technology.

4. Determine which activities, if any, you plan to conduct via the network other than computing. Sometimes, you don't know what you want to do until you know what you can do. You can include a game controller and entertainment centre, for instance.

In the UK, broadband Internet connections are generally fast (faster than in the US, in fact). The typical DSL connection might reach over 1 Mbps per second or even higher. It's unlikely that having multiple computers online and downloading videos or other files will degrade the quality of your connection. Nevertheless, if you plan to network four or more devices, you might give some thought to the bandwidth you have available, to make sure you don't overload your system and end up with all of your computers running sluggishly. If one of your grandchildren is downloading a 999 MB movie from a network where free video files are made available, such as BitTorrent, while another is sending 10 MB worth of digital images to a shared photo website such as Flickr, that will have an impact on network performance, especially when combined with your everyday web surfing activities.

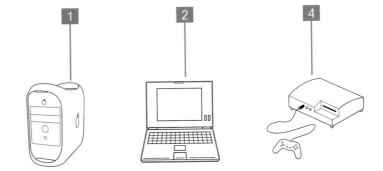

**Projecting the
number of
computers you
want to network
and their location
(cont.)**

5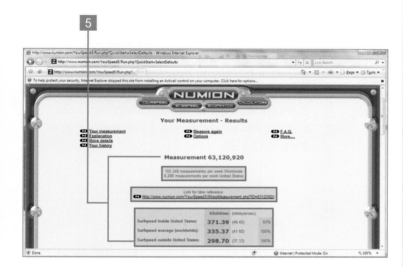

5 Do a speed test of your
network by going to the
Numion website
http://www.numion.com.
Make a note of the speed of
your current Internet
connection.

6 Consider the expected load on
your system. it can be difficult
to estimate this accurately, as
you can't be sure what every
member of your family is
going to be doing on the
Internet at any one time. But
ask yourself if you are likely to
be viewing videos,
downloading complex Adobe
Reader documents with lots of
images and embedded fonts,
or sending and receiving big
files or groups of files that are
more than 1 MB in size. If so,
you definitely need a high-
speed Internet connection, and
you need as much bandwidth
as you can get.

For your information

You want your wireless router to broadcast a signal to
all of the networked devices within your home's walls
but not beyond those walls. A special type of hacker
called a 'wardriver' exists who drives around
neighbourhoods looking for unsecured access points.
In addition, your neighbours may be able to 'see' your
network in their own wireless access software. Make
sure you secure your wireless network with encryption.

Positioning your router and networked devices

Once you have determined the goals and general configuration of your wireless network, you need to map out the number of computers and other devices you want to network. Ideally, with a wireless network you can position computers, game consoles and other such devices anywhere you want around your house. But in reality, you need to take walls, plumbing and other possible interference sources into consideration because they can affect wireless radio signals. You also have to take the distance between computers into account. If the distance between the router and one of the computers is 15–30 metres or more, you will probably have problems communicating with the network. And the more potentially interfering barriers you have between the router and the computer, the slower your data will move. That's why it's important to map out the network and your devices. Note any physical obstacles that will slow down network performance: ceiling tiles, trees, coated glass (or glass with a wire mesh in it) or brick walls.

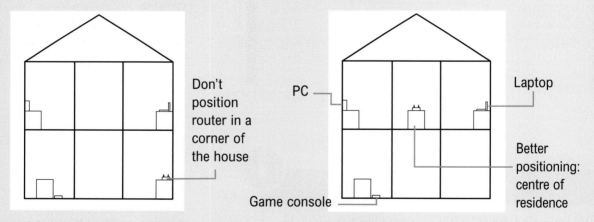

Don't position router in a corner of the house

PC

Laptop

Better positioning: centre of residence

Game console

Positioning the router at one corner of the house makes it difficult for users at the other end to receive the signal.

Positioning the router at a central location makes it easier to receive a strong signal from any location.

Did you know?

Positioning your wireless router in the open air and high up in a room – and away from appliances that emit radio signals – can dramatically improve network performance. I had a friend whose Internet connection was slow and intermittent because the wireless router was positioned in the kitchen directly under a microwave oven. When I moved the wire out and up near the ceiling of the room, performance improved dramatically.

Get to know Wi-Fi protocols

In order to understand wireless communications, you need to know something about radio frequencies. Computers and wireless routers communicate by means of radio signals that travel through the air in the same way that FM or AM radio signals travel from a transmitter to a radio in your car or home.

Different wireless technologies are able to transmit different maximum distances. You need to pay attention to the fine print on the documentation that comes with the devices you purchase, so you know how far apart you can position your computers.

Of course nothing ever stays the same. Wireless network standards are changing frequently along with the popularity of the technology.

The 'alphabet soup' of network protocols designed by the Institute of Electrical and Electronics Engineers (IEEE) can be confusing. The most important thing to do, however, is to make sure the Wi-Fi certification logo is present when you make the purchase hardware. I know I promised to not say 'Wi-Fi,' but bear with me just this once.

If you are able to use the same Wi-Fi protocol to connect all your wireless devices, you can be sure they'll all communicate with one another (or, if they don't, you'll at least be able to eliminate the possibility of incompatible devices). You can still use a mixed network (one in which the devices use different protocols), but if they don't work together, you'll need to replace the incompatible ones.

7

What is a MAC address and why do you need to know about it?

Earlier in this book, you learned about Internet Protocol (IP) addresses. Another kind of address you need to know about is a Media Access Control (MAC) address. A MAC address is a complex-looking series of numbers that identifies a device on the network. The term MAC address is used less often than the term IP address, but it's just as important in terms of networking.

A MAC address is a 12-digit value that uniquely identifies a network adapter. You might hear a MAC address referred to as a *hardware address* or *physical address*. Such an address often takes this form:

MM:MM:MM:SS:SS:SS

In this type of address the first half identifies the manufacturer of the network adapter, while the second half represents the serial number that the manufacturer has given to the adapter. Here's an example:

00:A0:C9:23:S6:35

Here, the 00:A0:C9 part of the MAC address shows that the device was made by the Intel Corporation. The 23:S6:35 part is the unique serial number assigned to the device. In most networks the IP address is dynamic: it changes each time the device connects to the network. But the MAC address usually remains static.

Let's take a closer look at a network such as the one above. It uses IP. (And most home networks connect to the Internet and provide Internet access for individual computers, so they do use IP addressing.) The point I'm trying to make is that a map is maintained between a device's IP address and its MAC address. That map is known as an ARP table. In case you want to impress your friends, you can file away the following extra titbit of information: Dynamic Host Control Protocol (DHCP) also uses MAC addresses to assign IP addresses to networked devices.

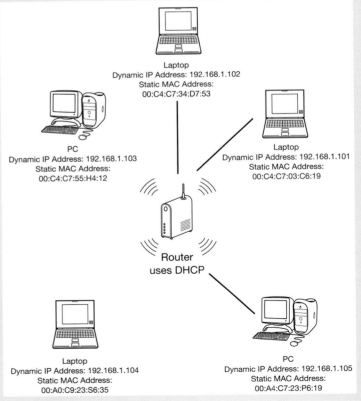

Laptop
Dynamic IP Address: 192.168.1.102
Static MAC Address:
00:C4:C7:34:D7:53

PC
Dynamic IP Address: 192.168.1.103
Static MAC Address:
00:C4:C7:55:H4:12

Laptop
Dynamic IP Address: 192.168.1.101
Static MAC Address:
00:C4:C7:03:C6:19

Router
uses DHCP

Laptop
Dynamic IP Address: 192.168.1.104
Static MAC Address:
00:A0:C9:23:S6:35

PC
Dynamic IP Address: 192.168.1.105
Static MAC Address:
00:A4:C7:23:P6:19

Features you will find in wireless access points

In the course of your shopping for Wi-Fi networking equipment, you might hear the salesperson use the term 'access point'. Don't be confused. An access point is merely a special type of router: hardware that acts as a gateway between the Internet and your home network.

An access point is used as a bridge between a set of computers on a wireless network and an access point, such as a hub, on an Ethernet network. That means that your ISP's Internet connection is shared by the Ethernet network and the wireless network at the same time. Because the antenna on a wireless access point is much stronger than the usual antenna on a router, an access point is an excellent tool for extending an Internet connection over a large area. The reason you seldom see access points on home networks is because a single router that can handle both wireless and Ethernet connections usually does the trick.

7

Getting what you need to go wireless

Introduction

Setting up a home network is a step-by step-process – and that applies to wireless networks, which are the most popular types around these days. In the previous chapter, you took the first step toward going wireless: you determined how many computers you need to network, and you mapped out where they need to be located. In this chapter, you'll assemble a shopping list of essential hardware items you will need. This might seem surprising, because one of the primary reasons for choosing a wireless network is freedom from hardware – most notably, freedom from Ethernet or other cables. But you have to purchase at least a bit of essential hardware in order to get your wireless network up and running.

Although the main topic of this book is setting up a computer network, this chapter has a bonus for those of you who like to be footloose and fancy-free. You'll learn about other devices that give you network access (that is, access to the Internet or to your own files) while you're on the go. With a Wi-Fi phone or PDA you can get online from anywhere you roam. So make sure your passport is valid because by following some simple tasks you'll be able to get online without a wire from any location where you need Internet access. With a little advance planning, you can configure your wireless network easily at home or away.

What you'll do

Choose a wireless-enabled laptop

Determine whether or not you need a network adapter

Purchase an external wireless network adapter

Improve your laptop's wireless performance

Prepare to buy a Wi-Fi phone

Know what you need to buy a Wi-Fi PDA

Add Wi-Fi to your desktop

Buy a wireless router/ access point

Choosing a wireless-enabled laptop

Tips for shopping for laptops

1. When you're shopping for laptops, pay attention to the type of protocol supported by the network card. The protocol is a set of communications instructions that determines how quickly the device can send and receive information; it begins with 802. Your goal is to find the fastest available.

2. Another criterion for choosing a network card is the bandwidth. Most wireless adapters use the 2.4 GHz band.

3. Connect to discussion groups and see if anyone is complaining of problems with Internet access for the computer you are considering.

4. After you buy your machine, test it out right away in the location where you want to use it. If you're not happy, return it immediately. Most retail stores will let you take back a computer within seven days of purchase and get a full refund.

I recently had a discussion with my father (who is several decades over 50) about the best type of computer for going online. His impression is that a desktop computer – a machine with a separate monitor (or screen) and a separate box for the processor is the best choice. Not necessarily, I told him. Laptops obviously have the advantage of being easy to carry around. But what might not be so obvious is that they have all the computing power of desktop models.

Plus, you'll almost certainly get a wireless network adapter installed with any new laptop you buy. But when you're comparing notes with others who have laptops, you learn that all wireless cards aren't created equal. How do you choose the best wireless card for your needs?

Did you know?

There are a couple of downsides with using your laptop just as it is when you get it out of its box: the monitor and keyboard are smaller than on a desktop. Some people have trouble getting used to the touch pad (that rectangular area just below the keyboard), where you use your finger instead of a mouse to make selections on screen. But you can always buy a USB mouse and plug it in to your laptop. You can even buy an extra monitor if you find it hard to look at the small screen.

But before you spend money on a bigger monitor, check out Windows Vista's Zoom controls: most applications have a zoom slider in the bottom right-hand corner of the screen that lets you make everything bigger and easier to read with just a couple of mouse clicks.

8

Determining whether or not you need a network adapter

1. Click **Start**.
2. Click **Computer**.
3. Click **System properties.**
4. Click **Device Manager**.
5. When a User Account Control dialogue box appears, click **Continue**.

In order to get on the Internet wirelessly, your computer needs to be equipped with a network adapter (also sometimes known as a network card). This device contains a small-scale receiver and transmitter that communicates with a wireless router. You don't need to buy a network adapter if you have one already but how do you know if you have one? You won't necessarily see a rectangular device plugged into a port on your computer with a little label on it that says 'Wireless Network Adapter'. You might have such a card installed inside your computer, but there's no way of seeing it unless you open up the housing (which I don't recommend).

You can 'look inside' your computer to see what's installed, however. This is a useful technique for discovering what hardware you have and to track down any hardware that might not be functioning properly at any given time.

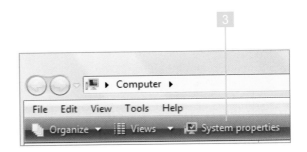

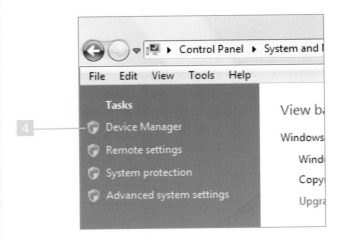

6 Click the plus sign (+) next to Network adapters.

7 Look at the network adapters listed and see if you have one that says 'wireless' and one of the 802.11n wireless protocol types listed. This is your wireless network adapter.

8 Make sure you don't have a red X or a warning sign icon to the left of the wireless adapter's name. If your icon looks like the one shown in the accompanying image, that means it is functioning properly.

9 Click the **Close** box to close the Device Manager window.

What does it mean if you don't see a wireless adapter listed? It means you need to purchase one by following the steps in the next task.

Purchasing an external wireless network adapter

1. Remove or disable your current network adapter as described in the next task.

2. Plug your USB adapter into one of your computer's USB ports. The Belkin G USB Wireless Network Adapter is shown right.

If your laptop's built-in adapter performs poorly or doesn't have a network card, consider purchasing an external USB wireless adapter. (If you are using a desktop computer, it might not have a wireless adapter at all. Many desktops are set up so they use wired Ethernet networks, but they don't have wireless capability. That requires you to buy a wireless adapter for them if that's how you want to get online.)

USB wireless adapters are especially good because you simply plug them into one of your computer's USB ports to get them up and running. You might have to also install software on a CD-ROM that comes with the device. But this only takes a few minutes. Other wireless adapters come in the form of a card that you have to install by opening your desktop computer and inserting it in a special hardware add-on slot. The USB adapter is obviously easier to use.

USB routers can also perform better than internal network adapters because they include antennas that communicate better with your router. Often, the problem is not that the router can't reach your adapter but that the adapter can't transmit signals back to the router.

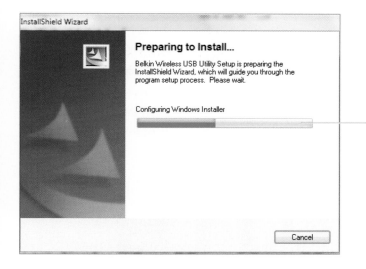

BELKIN. | Wireless G USB Network Adapter

Starting installation...

SETUP UTILITY | install | manual | support | exit

3

InstallShield Wizard

Preparing to Install...

Belkin Wireless USB Utility Setup is preparing the InstallShield Wizard, which will guide you through the program setup process. Please wait.

Configuring Windows Installer

4

Cancel

Purchasing an external wireless network adapter (cont.)

3 Insert the CD that came with the device in your computer's CD-ROM drive and click **install** (or a similar command) to begin installation.

4 Configure the adapter by following the installation wizard's instructions.

8

Did you know?

When you purchase a USB network adapter, you should take the same wireless network protocols into account. But don't expect to achieve the maximum throughput listed in your specifications. If your adapter is rated for 11 Mbps, for instance, you might be lucky to get a speed of 5 or 6 Mbps in the 'real world'.

Improving your laptop's wireless performance

Before you purchase add-on wireless antennas or new network adapters, 'look inside' your computer once again and try changing your network adapter's internal settings. Some adapters, in an attempt to save power and extend battery life, will limit the wireless card's transmission power. By adjusting this feature, you might just be able to improve performance in a matter of minutes and save yourself time and money in the bargain.

1 Click the **Start** button on the taskbar and choose **Computer**.

2 Click **System properties**.

3 Click **Device Manager**.

4 If a User Account Control dialogue box appears, click **Continue**.

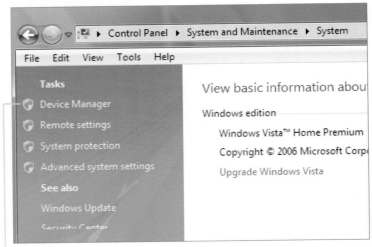

For your information

If you can't find the power management settings for your card, there are several possible solutions to the puzzle. It may mean that your wireless card doesn't support power management, or perhaps you don't have the latest drivers for your wireless adapter. The thing to do is to look for recent drivers from your laptop manufacturer or the manufacturer of your wireless adapter. Once you install the newest drivers, repeat the preceding steps to see if performance improves.

Improving your laptop's wireless performance (cont.)

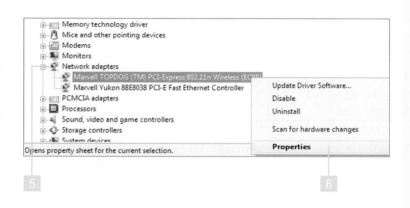

5 Click the plus sign next to **Network adapters**.

6 Right-click your wireless network adapter and choose **Properties** from the context menu.

7 Click the **Power Management** tab.

8 Disable the option that attempts to manage the power used by the network card. Don't tick the box allowing the device to wake your computer.

9 Click **OK**.

10 Test your wireless signal strength. Hopefully what was weak is now improved.

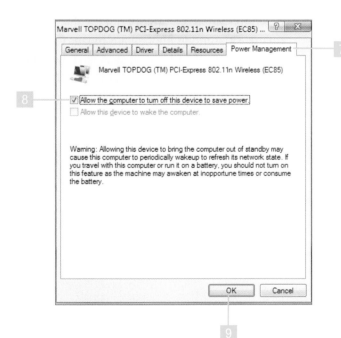

Buying a Wi-Fi phone

Wi-Fi isn't just for Internet access in fixed locations such as homes, businesses, schools and coffee shops. A relatively new device called a Wi-Fi phone lets you make a phone call to anyone in the world as long as you are within the range of a wireless network. It can reduce the cost of international phone calls. You might also be able to call from locations where you wouldn't normally get service, such as the underground.

VoIP phones

Wi-Fi phones come in two varieties. The first is designed to provide phone service via Voice over Internet Protocol (VoIP) providers such as Skype and Vonage. VoIP lets you make phone calls over the Internet rather than a mobile phone network or the traditional land-based phone networks. Skype is software you can install on your computer that lets you use your computer as a phone; you can talk to other individuals using a microphone and either a headset or a built-in speaker. Vonage adapts your existing broadband Internet connection so you can make phone calls over the Internet. Many Wi-Fi phones are set up to let you make calls using Skype.

Dual-mode phones

The problem with Wi-Fi phones is simple: Wi-Fi 'hotspots' aren't found everywhere. If you're in your home and you have wireless access, you can make a phone call. If you're near a coffee shop that is a Wi-Fi hotspot, you can make a phone call. But if you're in your car or walking down the street, you might not be able to get online. Dual-mode phones are meant to remedy this problem. If wireless access isn't available, a dual-mode phone will connect to a mobile phone network so you can make a call.

Buying a Wi-Fi PDA

A personal digital assistant (PDA) might be something your children or grandchildren use for business. But there's no reason why you can't 'wow' them by whipping out your own PDA and recording future appointments. Having your calendar in your hand will make it easy to remember birthdays, anniversaries and other special occasions.

When it comes to Personal Desk Assistants, otherwise known as 'palm' or 'handheld' devices, there are three options for connecting to the Internet: Bluetooth, Wi-Fi and GPRS (General Packet Radio Service). Bluetooth requires you to have a Bluetooth-compatible mobile phone. With GPRS, you can connect to the Internet and get your e-mail using your PDA, but you pay a monthly fee. With Wi-Fi, you can pick up your e-mail without the extra fee or the Bluetooth mobile phone. As long as

you're in range of a Wi-Fi network, you can go online and check your e-mail or send messages. This doesn't have to be an either/or decision, however. Many PDAs come with two or more of these features, so ask your salesperson lots of questions before you close the deal.

Wi-Fi PDAs tend to be more expensive than those without the ability to connect to the Internet. But they're worth the extra expense in terms of convenience and mobility. However, security is one potential downside. Zdnet.co.uk reports that a vulnerability in the 802.11 DSSS (direct-sequence spread spectrum) wireless protocol used by PDAs gives hackers the ability to intercept data being sent to or from the device. Read more about it at **http://news.zdnet.co.uk/communications/ 0,1000000085,39154656,00.htm**.

Adding Wi-Fi to your desktop

Your laptop probably came with a wireless card pre-installed. But suppose you don't have a laptop. Instead, you have a desktop computer: a box called a 'tower' that contains your ports, your disk drives and the accessories that keep your machine operating smoothly. You can however, add a wireless adapter to your desktop PC if it doesn't already have one. You have two options: add an internal PC card or add an external USB device.

Many older PCs don't include many USB ports. If you don't have any left, purchase a USB expansion hub, which will give you four more ports. You can then plug an external Wi-Fi antenna into the USB port (after installing the necessary software from the CD-ROM that comes with this device) so you can connect to your home wireless network.

Buying a wireless router/access point

When you head to the computer store to purchase a wireless router, you're probably thinking primarily about price. Although we all love to save money, there are a few other factors that should influence your decision.

Finding a compatible brand

The most popular brands for wireless routers (such as Netgear, Linksys and D-Link) are all good choices. But you might see a slightly higher performance if you stick to the same manufacturer as the network adapters installed in the computers on your network. **Vendors may also more thoroughly test compatibility with their own equipment. If you don't own any adapters (or newer laptops with built-in wireless), consider purchasing all of your Wi-Fi gear together from the same manufacturer.**

Considering bandwidth and performance

As you probably expect, the letters after the Wi-Fi protocol 802.11 can tip you off as far as the speed of the data that can be transmitted by a particular router. So you need to pay attention to those letters when you choose a router. Keep in mind that 802.11g, at 54 Mbps, has a far greater bandwidth than 802.11a devices, which have a top speed of 11 Mbps. But you can now find routers and network adapters that use the 802.11n protocol (100 Mbps) on Amazon.co.uk. Wireless routers are generally available from £50–70.

Find a good fit in size and style

You don't usually think of style and colour when you search for a wireless router. **But why not select an attractive addition to the decor that you will be proud to show family and friends? If you plan to install the router in a confined space, you'll be glad to know that they come in a variety of sizes and shapes. Finally, if you have a lot of trips scheduled, you'll want to look into 'travel router' products.**

Setting up your wireless network

Introduction

Congratulations: you've accomplished a great deal. You've already purchased the home network hardware you need and given some thought to the placement of your wireless router or access point. So now the big moment has arrived when you can start installing the hardware you need. But I'm not going to send you on a frantic search for screwdrivers, hammers, nail guns or other tools. Your more immediate tasks involve plugging things in as well as determining the right position for them in your home.

Wireless networks are easy to operate, as long as you take care to do the installation correctly. Don't try to do too many tasks at once. For instance, purchasing several home PCs and installing Windows Vista at the same time as adding wireless network adapters would confuse even an expert. Instead, make sure your laptops or PCs are up and running smoothly. That way, if you run into problems with your wireless connection, you'll know to blame the wireless hardware and not the computers. Also, make sure your broadband connection is functioning properly. Then you can undertake the tasks described in this chapter with the confidence that soon your wireless network will be humming.

What you'll do

Ensure your network is up and running

Collect your ISP's network data

Find your network card's physical address

Locate your router/access point

Reconfigure your router

Change your router's MAC address

Choose basic wireless settings

Purchase an external antenna

Making sure your network is up and running

Before you start adding wireless routers and network adapters, make sure all of your computers and your broadband connection are working they way they should be. If you already have a broadband connection and one or more computers in place, you can skip the following steps. But if you are starting from scratch, it pays to begin in a systematic and thorough way.

1 Make sure your broadband connection is working correctly.

2 Add one PC or laptop to the network.

3 Make sure this PC is connected to the Internet

4 Add a second PC or laptop to the network.

5 Make sure all devices can see one another by clicking the start button and choosing **Network**. In the **Network** dialogue box, the connected devices should be displayed. You now know your Internet connection and local network connectivity are functioning correctly.

6 You should now be ready to begin adding wireless connectivity to your home network as described in the tasks that follow.

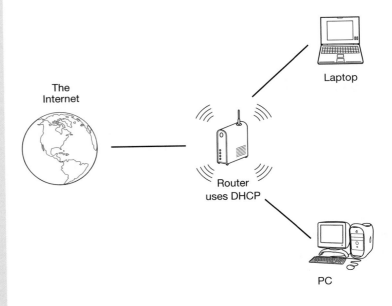

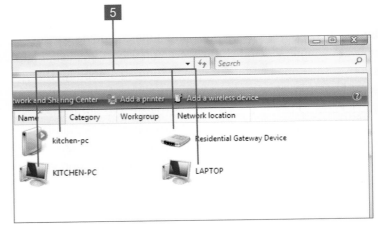

Before you plug in your router and start communicating wirelessly, you need to gather and write down some essential information about your Internet connection and the current network card you're using. You may need your notes when troubleshooting later on, so make sure you remember where you put them.

Collecting your ISP's network data

1 Call your ISP's technical support staff and ask for the following:

- your IP address (it will take the form 67.111.89.4 – four numbers separated by dots)

- the IP address of your ISP's DNS server. (You will probably get two addresses; one is an alternative in case the first is unavailable.)

- whether or not your ISP uses Dynamic Host Configuration Protocol (DHCP).

2 If you'd rather get the information yourself, begin by clicking the **Start** button on the taskbar. Then type **Command Prompt** and press **Enter**.

3 When the command prompt window opens, type **ipconfig /all** (make sure there is a blank space before the forward slash (/).

4 Press **Enter**.

5 Scroll down and note the relevant information, as displayed here.

9

Finding your network card's physical address

If you connect to the Internet through a single computer with a network adapter, get the MAC address (also known as a physical address) of that adapter. Some ISPs use the physical address as a security measure. That's because if a computer with an address different from yours connects to the Internet using the ISP's gateway, it might think your connection is being stolen. If your router lets you change its MAC address, you should match the MAC address of the network card you already use.

1 Follow steps 1–4 in the preceding task.

2 Scroll down in the Command Prompt window and find the name of your network adapter.

3 Write down the address, which will take the form 04-00-33 2E-05

DHCP

IP addresses

DNS addresses

See also

To actually change the MAC address assigned to your router, see 'Changing your router's MAC address' later in this chapter.

Installing your router/access point software

The best and first step to follow in installing a wireless router is to read your manufacturer's instructions and follow them closely. In many cases, you won't have to do much: your router might detect your IP address settings automatically and configure themselves. But if they don't, you'll need to do the configuration manually. See the note above about reading the directions! Then insert the CD-ROM that comes with your wireless router.

When you get the prompt from the router setup program, connect the router to your broadband modem with an Ethernet cable. When the software prompts you again, begin providing essential bits of information, such as:

- SSID, the service set identifier
- channel
- WEP or WPA keys
- password
- MAC address
- IP address
- local IP address
- subnet address
- PPPoE

The tasks that follow will discuss each of these bits of information in turn.

9

For your information

This chapter uses the term 'router' to describe the hardware that connects to your broadband modem and distributes the connection to the Internet to the different computers in your home. But don't get confused if you see a reference to an 'access point' or to a 'base station'. Those are just other names for the same thing.

Locating your router/access point software

No matter what it's called, your device will come with a CD-ROM that contains configuration software. You can install this software on any of the computers on your network. Take your pick. As long as your computer is connected to the network, it doesn't even matter whether your connection is wired or wireless. When you're ready, insert the disk in your computer's CD-ROM drive and follow these steps.

1 When the AutoPlay dialogue box appears, click **Run SetupWizard.exe** (the exact file name will differ depending on the router you choose).

2 When a User Account Control dialogue box appears, click **Allow**.

3 When the Welcome screen appears, click **Setup** (again, the wording may differ depending on the device you are configuring).

? Did you know?

A secure password consists of at least six or seven characters, contains a mixture of numerals and characters, and is not a recognisable word in the dictionary. If you forget your password, you'll need to reset your router and configure it from scratch. If you need help, you can consult your user manual (probably contained on your setup CD) and/or call a helpful person who works for the manufacturer of the router.

Locating your router/access point software (cont.)

4 The next screen of this wizard tells you not to plug your router in as the setup program will automatically detect your computer's settings and use them for configuration. Click **Next**.

5 Wait while the setup program automatically detects your settings.

6 Plug the router's Internet port into your broadband modem when prompted to do so.

7 If the setup program does not work or you need to manually configure your router, follow the steps in subsequent tasks.

9

Reconfiguring your router

What happens if you change your ISP? It happens all the time. A friend of mine had a contract for many years with a popular access company but, after a week-long service outage, he cancelled and chose a much larger company. You might also decide to switch if you want to combine cable service and Internet access, to save money for instance.

When my friend switched, he needed technical help with his router. What was the problem? In his case, his router was simply incompatible with his new ISP's system. More commonly, though, you'll need to change the IP address information that your router uses to give your home computers access to the Internet. Log in to your router's configuration utility and access the tab that lets you perform 'basic setup' tasks (for the Linksys WRT54G this is, literally, called the Basic Setup tab). Then replace the current information shown below with the new information given to you by your ISP.

1 Choose your connection type (in this case, **Static IP**). Chances are good that your connection is one of these options:

- Automatic Configuration – DHCP. This is the most common setup; your ISP does not assign you a specific IP address, but your router uses DHCP to assign private IP addresses.

- Static IP. If you pay extra, your ISP might assign you a static IP address – one that you can use to identify your computer on the Internet. You don't really need a static IP address unless you intend to run a web server on your computer, in which case you need to have a stable, static address so visitors can find your website easily.

- PPTP. Point-to-Point Tunnelling Protocol is used by some ISPs in Europe. Ask your ISP if this type of connection is in use. If so, you'll need to obtain a username and password.

Reconfiguring your router (cont.)

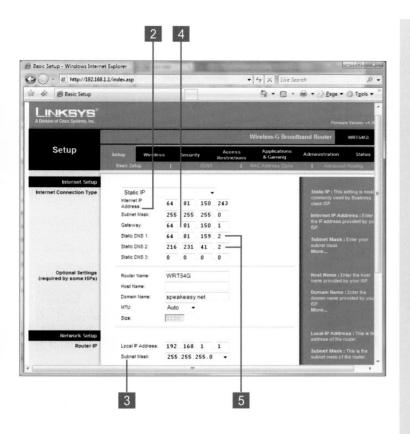

- PPPoE. Some ISPs use Point-to-Point Protocol over Ethernet. Ask your ISP if you should choose this option. You'll need to enter a username and password for this option, too.

2 Type your router's IP address. Even though your home computers have private IP addresses, your router needs to have a public one so it can send and receive data with sites on the Internet. Your ISP will supply you with this address.

3 Subnet Mask. This complicated-looking name tells another computer about the size of your network. Type the subnet mask here as supplied by your ISP.

4 Gateway. This is the IP address of the webserver you use to connect to your ISP.

5 DNS addresses. These are the addresses of your ISP's Domain Name Server. This server uses the Domain Name Service (DNS) to resolve domain names like pearson.com into IP addresses like 195.69.212.200. You'll probably be given two DNS addresses: a primary and a secondary one.

9

Did you know?

Every computer on the Internet has an IP address – a series of four or six numbers separated by dots that identifies the computer so information can be routed to it. It's like a street address that the post office uses to deliver mail. Private IP addresses are in the range 192.168.x.x. This address range was set aside for use with local networks. Private IP addresses were originally created because regular IPv4 addresses were running out. (A new IPv6 address system now makes sure there are lots of addresses available.) Public IP addresses, in contrast, can be used on public networks such as the Internet.

Changing your router's MAC address

As stated earlier in this chapter, some ISPs restrict access to their DNS servers to only specified computers with specific MAC addresses. You can change the MAC address of your router to match that of your computer, however. You do this in your router's configuration screen. Look for a tab named Setup or something similar. (Search your router's instructions for the subject 'Mac Address Clone' and you'll find the correct location.)

1 Click the **Setup** tab.

2 Click **MAC Address Clone**.

3 Click **Enable**.

4 Type the MAC address of the computer that you want to clone here.

5 Click **Clone your PC's MAC**.

6 Click **Save Settings**.

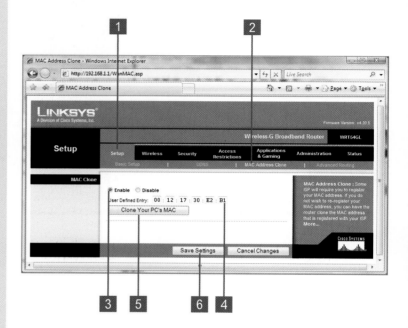

Did you know?

You don't necessarily have to clone your PC's MAC address. This is necessary only if your ISP requires you to register a MAC address before you can access the Internet.

Some of the most important wireless settings you can configure are listed under a heading such as 'basic wireless settings'. These settings control what mode your router uses to communicate with network adapters around your house, the name of your network, and whether the router should broadcast its name. They are important not only for the security of your network but also for the level of performance it reaches.

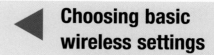

Choosing basic wireless settings

Choose the network mode

1 Click the **Wireless** tab.

2 Select one of the options from the Wireless Network Mode drop-down list:

■ Mixed. Choose this option if the router and network adapters on your wireless network use different network protocols – for instance, Wireless-G and 802.11b.

■ G-Only or B-Only. Choose the appropriate option if all of the devices on your network use the same network protocol.

■ Disable. If none of the devices on your network uses G or B, choose this option.

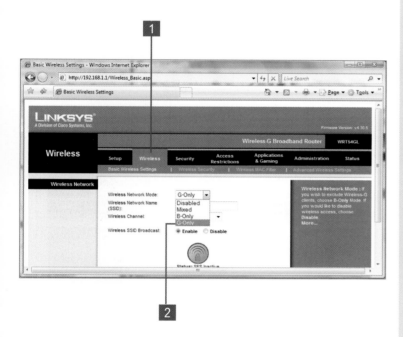

9

Did you know?

If you're looking for the best wireless router name, check out **http://compnetworking.about.com/**. At the Oh Punk! blog, people have been discussing the names (SSIDs) of wireless network routers. Most will agree that 'default' is a really boring name. 'Pookie' is a little bit better, but not much!

Choosing basic wireless settings (cont.)

Choose your wireless SSID

3 Type your wireless network name (SSID). This is the name assigned to your wireless network. It's the name all of your computers will use when they connect to your router (and, by extension the network and the Internet). The name should be short, easy to remember, and not too silly.

Choose a wireless channel

4 Choose a wireless channel from the list of available channels.

5 Click **Reset Security**.

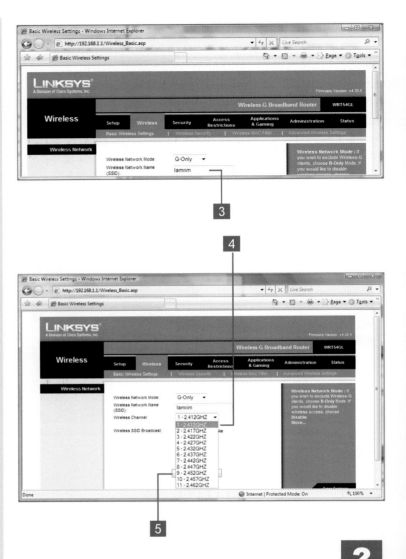

Did you know?

The typical low-cost router has antennas to transmit the wireless signal throughout your house, as well as several ports. If your signal isn't strong, don't immediately assume you need to string Ethernet cables or buy a new router. You can save a few pounds by purchasing a low-cost USB antenna that plugs into one of your computer's USB ports. If you have a computer that is located in a room far away from the main router, a secondary antenna can help connect to it.

I'm sure I'm not the only one who has tried to improve TV reception by twisting a wire clothes hanger into a make-shift antenna. I recommend that you buy an add-on antenna instead of making your own if you are unhappy with the performance of your laptop's built-in wireless adapter. That often works better than buying a USB adapter. Most internal network adapters included with laptops come with omni-directional antennas. They transmit a signal in all directions around the computer. If your router is on another floor of your house or behind a wall, the signal might not reach it because half of the signal is being sent in the wrong direction. A simple antenna directs your adapter's signal to the computer in one direction, improving communication dramatically. Some antennas connect to your wireless router and increase the signal in that direction as well.

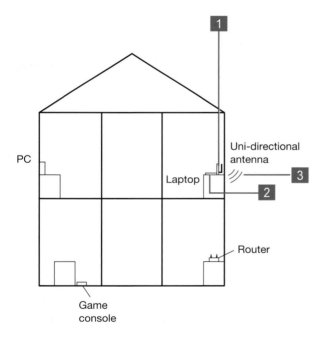

Purchasing an external antenna

1 Obtain a high-gain antenna, such as the Hawking HAI7SIP.

2 Plug the antenna into your computer's USB port or into your router.

3 Point the antenna in the direction of the router in your home.

Did you know?

Here's a good basis for comparison. The Hawking HA15SC Hi-Gain Wireless Corner antenna is designed to connect to your wireless access point or router. It sits in a corner of a room and broadcasts a 15 dBi signal (far higher than the standard 2 dBi signal). The Hawking is available from **http://www.amazon.co.uk**. A 7 dBi version, the Hawking HAI7SIP, is also available from the same site.

9

Securing your home network

Introduction

I probably don't have to tell you about the importance of security in relation to the Internet. Chances are you've heard of spam, viruses and cases in the news in which credit card and other personal information has been stolen by hackers who either break into insecure websites or trick people into giving out information. What you need to know, in relation to this book, is the fact that security becomes even more important when you network two or more computers so they can share information and go online. First I'll give you the bad news about things that can go wrong, but then I'll give you ways to protect yourself, your information and your computer.

What you'll do

Understand security dangers threatening your home network

Choose wireless network passwords

Choose a wireless security method

Assign your network a password and security method

Disable ad-hoc network connections

Secure your network with Windows Firewall

Enable your firewall on your router

Run a firewall/anti-virus program

Set access restrictions for your housemates

Set up a DMZ

Establish application and gaming restrictions

Rename your network

Understanding the security dangers

When you create a home network, you dramatically improve access to information for yourself and other members of your household. But that access goes in two directions. When you open up a gateway so others can access the Internet, you also give unscrupulous users on the Internet a way to access your computers. My 15-year-old daughter had her computer briefly 'taken over' by hackers who placed a malicious program called a Trojan horse on her system, which she then unknowingly downloaded along with other software. That's only one way in which unauthorised individuals can infiltrate your network. They regularly gain access to unsecured wireless networks or to computers that simply haven't been protected with strong passwords – or with any passwords at all. Home networks need security systems just as much as corporate ones; the unauthorised traffic resulting from computers that have been taken over and turned into 'zombies', sending out spam e-mail or launching attacks on other computers, slows down the network for everyone who uses the Internet.

What are the dangers?

You might well ask: why would a hacker want to gain access to a home computer? After all, it's easy to understand why computers in the government or the military would be attractive. Corporate computer networks store lots of customer information, such as credit card numbers, that can be used by criminals. But you probably don't store information that's so valuable. Or do you?

Chances are you do have some passwords that would be of interest to hackers, such as the ones you use to do your online banking or to pay your credit cards online. But that's not the only reason why a hacker would love to be the spider and make you into the fly. Your computer itself, not to mention your Internet connection, are also of interest. Hackers frequently assume control of computers that are online 24/7 because they have dedicated broadband connections and are never turned off by their owners. They can use the machines to launch coordinated attacks on large-scale corporate computers: by flooding a server with connection requests made by thousands of computers around the world, the server is overwhelmed and unable to function.

A 2005 report by the security firm Symantec said that the UK led the world in 'zombie' home computers that had been hijacked by hackers – 25 percent of such computers were located in Britain (**http://news.bbc.co.uk/2/hi/technology/4369891.stm**).

If your system is compromised by a remote user, you could be in big trouble. I don't want to scare you, but I do need to make you aware of some of the dangers. They include the following:

- **Identity theft**. Hackers who gain access to your identification numbers can assume your identity and make unauthorised purchases.

What are the dangers? (cont.)

■ **Credit card theft**. Your credit card numbers can be stolen, with obvious consequences.

■ **Loss of functionality**. A computer that has been taken over by a hacker is slow to respond. It might barely respond to your mouse clicks or menu commands because it is busy performing other processes of which you are not even aware.

■ **Loss of privacy**. Hackers might install programs that track your keystrokes, enabling them to steal passwords and other information you type, such as your e-mail messages and financial records.

■ **Reduced performance**. If someone freeloads on your wireless network, they can download movies or perform other functions that slow down performance for you and other members of your household.

A special breed of hacker seeks to perform the last objective listed above. 'Wardrivers' drive around, looking for unsecured wireless networks they can connect to. Once on the network, they can use 'packet sniffing' software to detect your passwords, or they can run commands that might harm your operating system.

An article on the Out-Law.com website reports that many wardrivers in London mark spots where they can gain wireless access with chalk so others know a connection is available (**http://www.out-law. com/page-3443**).

10

Choosing wireless network passwords

If you have a home wireless network, you need to protect it by choosing a wireless security protocol and passwords. Wired Equivalent Privacy (WEP) is an older security protocol that was developed before the Wi-Fi Alliance's membership had agreed on a uniform method for treating passwords. WEP comes in two varieties: 64-bit and 128-bit security. In other words, the password you enter is converted by WEP into a complete 64-bit or 128-bit key. The decision of whether to use WEP or a newer protocol such as Wi-Fi Protected Access (WPA) depends on your network adapters and other wireless hardware: if they all support WEP, that's the protocol you should choose.

On the other hand, WEP is far from the most secure method of encrypting data that is transmitted wirelessly. WPA, which was developed in 2003, has many advantages over WEP. WEP uses longer keys and more complex encryption methods than WPA. It also manages keys more effectively, and has more effective ways to check the integrity of messages. WPA is such a strong choice that it might be the only option listed on your wireless network:

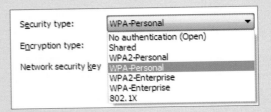

As you can see from the list, WPA comes in several varieties. You may feel like you're staring at a bowl full of alphabet soup, but don't lose your appetite. The original WPA uses Temporal Key Integrity Protocol (TKIP) with Message Integrity Check (MIC) to verify messages and keys. It also authenticates others on the network using the Mutual Pre-Shared Key (PSK) method. WPA2 uses also uses PSK, but uses Advanced Encryption Standard (AES) to encrypt data transmissions. On top of that, WPA comes in two certification modes: Enterprise and Personal. As a result, there are four options: WPA Personal, WPA Enterprise, WPA2 Personal, and WPA2 Enterprise. The Personal option is designed for small office and home environments so that's the one I recommend that you should choose. Since AES is a newer and more advanced encryption scheme than TKIP, it's a good choice as well.

The box above described, in general, differences between WEP and WPA as well as the different varieties of the WPA encryption method. Once you understand the options, you need to see which method Windows is currently using to protect your wireless communications, and to choose a new security scheme if necessary.

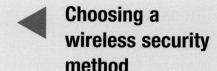

Choosing a wireless security method

1 Click the **Start** button on the taskbar.

2 Choose **Network**.

3 Click **Network and Sharing Center**.

4 Click **View status**.

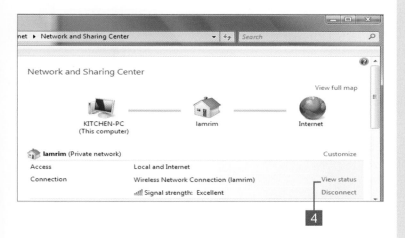

Choosing a wireless security method (cont.)

5 Click **Wireless Properties**.

6 Click the **Security** tab.

7 Choose a security type.

8 Choose an encryption type.

9 Click **OK**.

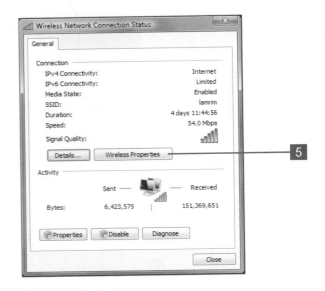

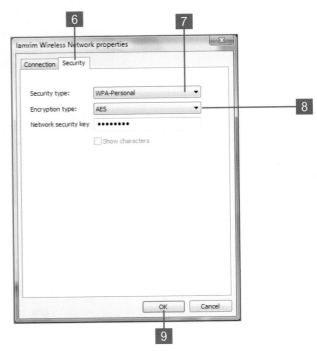

If you've ever shopped around for wireless networks, you'll know some are labelled as 'Unsecured' and others are protected by security. This simply means that you need to enter a password to gain access to the secured networks. The simplest and most obvious way to protect your wireless network, then, is to assign a password to it. Yet, many computer users fail to do this until they have had a security breach of some sort. Prevent trouble by taking a minute to make your network secure. At the same time, you can choose one of the encryption methods described earlier in this chapter.

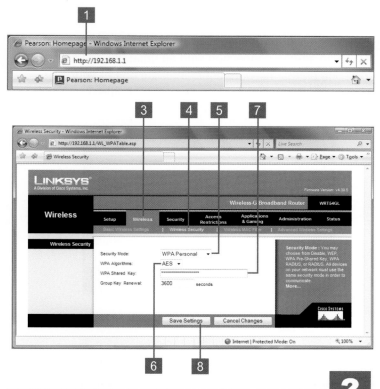

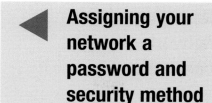

Assigning your network a password and security method

10

1 Connect to your wireless router or access point by entering 192.168.1.1 in your browser's Address box and pressing **Enter**.

2 Sign in with your router's username and password and click **OK**.

3 Click **Wireless**.

4 Click **Wireless Security**.

5 Choose a security method (WPA Personal or Enterprise, or WPA2 Personal or Enterprise).

6 Choose an encryption scheme (AES or TKIP).

7 Type a password for your network.

8 Click **Save Settings**.

Did you know?

By following this task and the preceding one, you have secured your network with encryption at two levels: at the router level and at the operating system level. The Group Key Renewal setting applies to the WPA security method. It changes the group key periodically for extra security. Don't worry about the default setting, which is probably either 1800 or 3600 seconds: there's no reason to change it.

Disabling ad-hoc network connections ▶

1 Single-click the wireless connection icon in your System Tray.

2 Choose **Network and Sharing Center**.

3 Click **View status**.

You've probably heard of an ad-hoc committee or solution, or maybe you've even participated in an ad-hoc parade or demonstration. When we're talking computers, an ad-hoc connection is one that is established only for a single session and not on a regular basis.

Sometimes this is good. Such connections are useful for laptops that you take to locations outside the home, such as wireless hotspots, where you need to connect to the Internet using wireless networks other than your own. But other times it can be bad. For desktop PCs that never move out of your house, ad-hoc connections aren't needed. In fact, they represent a slight but significant security risk. If your computer makes an ad-hoc connection with an unauthorised network, someone on that network could infiltrate one of your computers. What's the bottom line? You should disable ad-hoc networking for your desktop PCs for extra security.

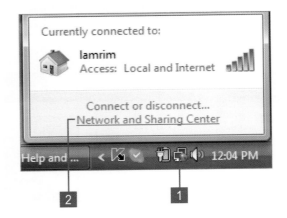

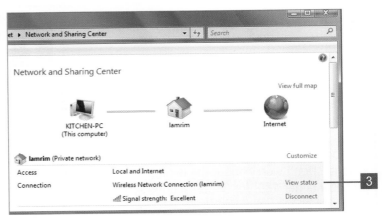

Disabling ad-hoc network connections (cont.)

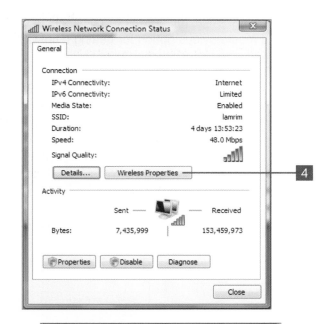

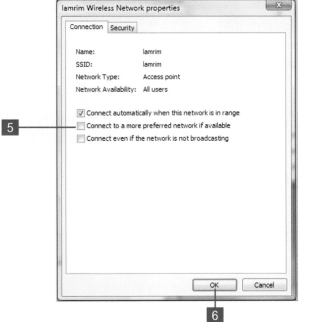

4 Click **Wireless Properties**.

5 Deselect the option 'Connect to a more preferred network if available'.

6 Click **OK**.

Securing your network with Windows Firewall

A firewall is hardware or software that monitors the traffic moving through a network gateway. It can be configured to block or allow traffic depending on certain criteria. For instance, if a random 'ping' message comes in from a remote site to your computer, the firewall can be configured to block it. If programs on your computer attempt to access remote sites without your knowledge, the firewall can block them as well. The first and most obvious option for getting a firewall in place is to use the one that comes with Windows.

1. Single-click the wireless connection icon in your System Tray.

2. Click **Network and Sharing Center**.

3. Click **Windows Firewall**.

4. Click **Turn Windows Firewall on or off**.

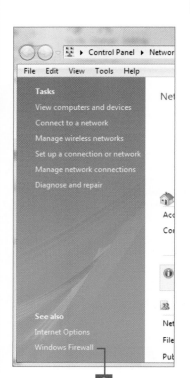

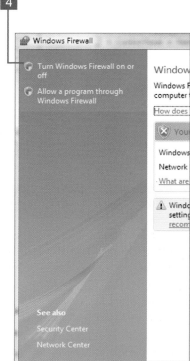

Did you know?

Ping is a networking utility that enables one computer to send small packets of digital information to other computers to which it is networked. Ping messages can be sent to computers on the Internet or on your home network. If you connect to a computer through Windows, you can 'ping' it to see if it is on the network.

5 When a User Account Control dialogue box appears, click **Continue**.

6 Click **On**.

7 Click **OK**.

For your information

If you run into problems connecting to the Internet or performing other functions while Windows Firewall is activated, it may be that a program you need is being blocked. To allow a program, click the **Exceptions** tab in the Windows Firewall Settings dialogue box shown here. Click **Add Program**, and then follow the directions to add the program to the list of 'allowed' applications. But first pause a moment to make sure the program you want to add is a legitimate one and not potentially malicious.

Enabling your firewall on your router

1. Enter 192.168.1.1 in your browser's Address box and press **Enter**.

2. Sign in with your username and password to access your router.

3. Click **Security**.

4. Click **Firewall** if necessary.

5. Click **Enable**.

6. Tick this box to prevent anonymous Internet users from 'pinging' or trying to contact your computer.

7. Tick this box to block out multicast data transmissions that are occasionally sent by your ISP.

8. Tick here to prevent your home networked computers from accessing any servers (webservers or e-mail servers) you have set up at home. This prevents hackers who have infiltrated your computers from accessing the servers as well.

9. Tick here to prevent attacks through port 113 on your computer.

10. Click **Save Settings**.

A router makes a perfect firewall because it acts as a gateway between the Internet and the computers on your home network. Virtually all routers/access points, whether they use Ethernet or function wirelessly, have a firewall function built into them. The only thing you have to do is to make sure your router is enabled to be a firewall and that in the process it won't block programs you need.

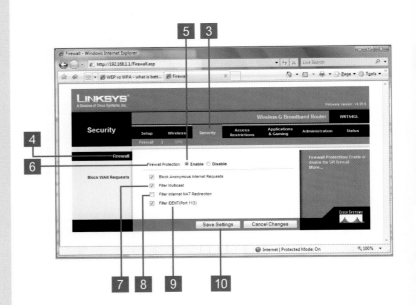

Did you know?

Port 113 was originally proposed to create a means for remote servers to identify automatically computers that were connecting to them; for instance, users attempting to connect to an FTP server. But hackers can easily exploit this port to gain anonymous access to your computer. That's why it's a good idea to prevent connection attempts on this port.

Your home network probably has a high-speed connection that is 'always on'. That could be either a DSL or a cable modem connection to the Internet. In any case, it presents a tempting target to hackers. One of the most effective ways to prevent unauthorised users from gaining access to your network is to install a third-party firewall and anti-virus program. This section isn't going to recommend a particular program, since several applications are effective (although you can see that this book's author uses Kaspersky Internet Security by Kaspersky Labs).

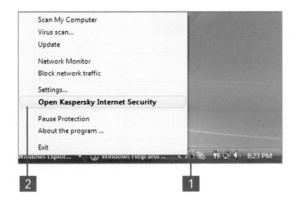

 Running a firewall/anti-virus program

1 Most firewall/anti-virus programs, like this one, can be accessed from an icon in the System Tray. Right-click the icon to view a menu full of actions it can perform.

2 Choose **Open...** to open the application

3 Click here to scan your computer for viruses and other malicious programs.

4 Click here to install new databases; updates are essential to keep up with the latest threats.

5 Click here to open the program's firewall.

10

Running a firewall/anti-virus program (cont.)

6 Click here to change the filtration level and rules for the firewall.

6

Did you know?

Some anti-virus programs give you a chance to try them out before you purchase them – without even having to install them on your computer. The Kaspersky Labs website (**http://www.kaspersky.com**), for instance, is one good example. Click the **Virus Scan** link near the top of the page. On the next page, click **Scan Now**, and follow the steps on subsequent pages to see if spyware and viruses are resident on your computer.

Having a router that you can use to control access to the Internet has many benefits. Not only can you limit access to outsiders, but you can exercise controls on those within your household as well. This is important if you are providing Internet access to children, grandchildren or other visitors and you don't want them going online at certain times of the day or week. It's your house, so you get to make the rules . . . right? Right!

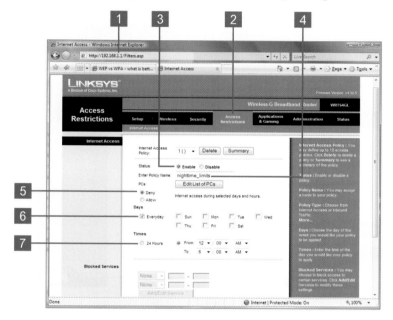

Restrict access times

1 Connect to your router by entering 192.168.1.1 as described in previous tasks.

2 Click **Access Restrictions**.

3 Click **Enable**.

4 Type a name for the policy you are creating.

5 Click **Deny** to deny access at certain times.

6 Choose the days on which the access policy will be in effect (or leave the default option, **Everyday**, selected).

7 Choose the times during which you want the policy to be in effect.

8 Click **Save Settings**.

Setting access restrictions for your housemates (cont.)

Restrict websites

9 Click **Enable**.

10 Click **Allow**.

11 Enter the URLs of websites you don't want members of your household to visit.

12 Enter keywords that describe content you don't want members of your household to see.

13 Click **Save Settings**.

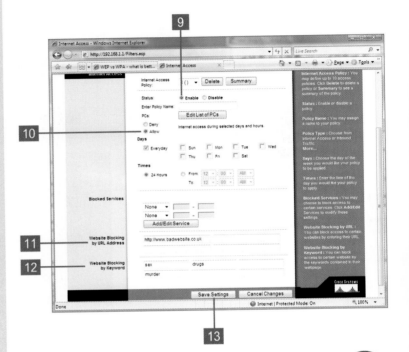

For your information

It's you're choice whether or not you name your policy, but it can be useful if you have multiple policies in place and you need to tell them apart. Be sure not to enter blank spaces in the policy name box; instead, use the underscore character between words.

A DMZ (demilitarised zone) is a computer or mini-network that lies between the Internet and the private network being protected. Users on the Internet are allowed access to the computer(s) in the DMZ but not the private network. You may want to configure one of your computers as a DMZ, especially if you, your children or grandchildren are using it for playing Internet games.

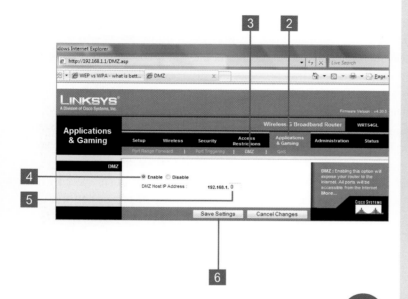

1 Connect to your router as described in preceding tasks in this chapter.

2 Click the **Applications & Gaming tab**.

3 Click **DMZ**.

4 Click **Enable**.

5 Enter the last part of the IP address of the computer that is to serve as the DMZ.

6 Click **Save Settings**.

10

For your information

Make sure you don't have any sensitive information on the computer designated as the DMZ. That should be easy to remember if you keep in mind that ports will be opened on the DMZ computer so game players can interact with it.

Setting application and gaming restrictions

Many games, especially those that allow you to play with others via the Internet, open up connections to your local network that can represent a security risk. You can use your router to restrict the games that those on your network can use so they don't unintentionally expose your network to hackers. In this sense, having a router to protect your home network is a big security asset. It's far more secure than a single computer connected directly to the Internet that is 'wide open' to outsiders because its owner is playing games online.

For instance, let's say that you or someone in your household is playing an online game that needs to use port 7000. You can use the Port Forwarding function in your router to make sure requests for port 7000 traffic go only to the computer that is playing that particular game. This protects the other computers on the network.

Other Application and Gaming Restrictions, such as port triggering and Quality of Service, let you control the amount of bandwidth a game is consuming and the number of ports used by each application. It's a way of preventing the game from overwhelming your system and slowing down performance for that computer and others on your home network.

Renaming your network

The name or SSID of your wireless network is probably one of the least important names you'll have to come up with in the course of networking. It's certainly not as important as the name of your computer or your workgroup, for instance.

On the other hand, choosing a clear name that is easy to remember and that you can divulge to others without blushing is always a good idea. If you have taken your laptop out 'roaming' and are looking for a wireless signal, you are probably familiar with the kinds of names others come up with. The most frequently used are:

- Netgear
- Default
- Linksys.

These are three default names assigned by the router manufacturers. The problem with them is that they are overused. If you don't bother to change the default name, when you attempt to connect to your own wireless network you may discover that one or more other networks in your vicinity share your same name.

Keep in mind that if guests stay at your home and ask for Internet access, you'll have to give them your SSID. A silly or naughty name can be embarrassing to provide to your children or grandchildren. On the other hand, you can also have fun and be creative with your SSID: if you're a Star Wars fan, consider R2D2, Obie-Wan or something similar.

10

Sharing your photos and other files

11

Introduction

Working at your computer doesn't need to be a solitary activity. It's often the most fun when you share the experience with others – when you look at a website or photos with family or friends. These days, you don't need to bring out heavy photo albums to pass around. What's even more exciting is that photos you have taken with a digital camera and saved as computer documents are only the most obvious files you can experience together. You can also make music clips, videos and word-processing documents available to others without having to print them out and carry them around or send them through the post.

One of the biggest advantages of setting up a home network, in fact, is the ability to share files. You and others in your household want to be able to view photo albums, read newsletters and share other information without having to carry around Flash drives or CDs. Once you have your computers and other devices networked and named, it's easy to share files. The key is to be able to share them *securely* – to set the system up so only approved individuals see the files they are supposed to see, without your neighbours or unauthorised users snooping in on your private information.

What you'll do

Activate File and Print Sharing

Fine-tune your file sharing settings

Set up a shared folder

Create user accounts and passwords

Review the pros and cons of file and print sharing

Understand user accounts and permissions

Share a password-protected resource

Set advanced sharing options

Adjust how your computer stores shared resources

Assign multiple sharing policies to the same resource

Locate your other network computers

Enable Network Discovery

Directly access a shared resource on Windows XP

Share a network drive

Activating File and Print Sharing

File and Print Sharing is a Windows service that isn't necessarily turned on by default. Once you turn on File and Print Sharing, other users on your network can see and make use of your files. The danger is that outsiders who are able to infiltrate your network can also see shared files. That's why you need to restrict what you share and use password protection for extra security.

1 Click the **Start** button on the taskbar.

2 Choose **Network**.

3 Click **Network and Sharing Center**.

4 Click **View status**.

5 Click **Properties**.

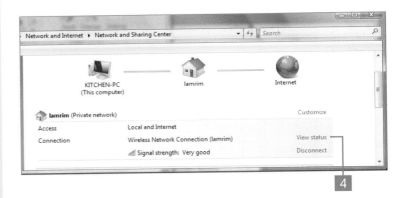

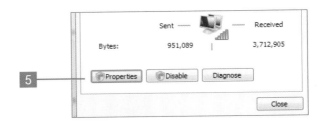

Activating File and Print Sharing (cont.)

6 When the User Account Control dialogue box appears, click **Continue**.

7 Make sure **File and Printer Sharing for Microsoft Networks** is ticked.

8 Click **OK**.

For your information

Make sure, in Network and Sharing Center, that your network is listed as private. If you have File and Print Sharing turned on, making the network private will make it harder for unauthorised users to see your computers.

Fine-tuning file sharing settings

In addition to the steps presented in the preceding task, the Network and Sharing Center window gives you another place to fine-tune file sharing settings. It's a window that does double duty. The upper half of the window handles networking information; the lower half contains a variety of file sharing options that you can use to control what you share and how you share it. In this task, you will create a shared folder that is available to everyone on the network without a password.

1. Open **Network and Sharing Center** as described in steps 1–3 of the preceding task.

2. Scroll down to the **Sharing and Discovery** options.

3. Click the arrow next to **File sharing**.

Fine-tuning file sharing settings (cont.)

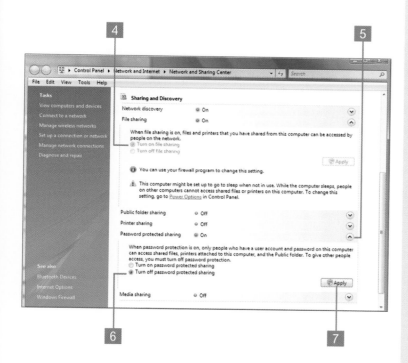

4 Make sure the **Turn on file sharing** button is selected.

5 Click the arrow next to **Password protected sharing**.

6 Click the button next to **Turn off password protected sharing**.

7 Click **Apply**.

11

Sharing your photos and other files 167

Setting up a shared folder

Okay, so now you've turned password protection off as described in the preceding task. What's next? Setting up a network share will create a shared folder that anyone can access. Obviously, you should not place sensitive files in this folder. There is no protection, after all. But this kind of setup gives you an easy way to get started, and you will set up password protected folders later on.

1 Click the **Start** button on the taskbar.

2 Choose **Computer**.

3 Open your disk drive.

4 Click **File**, click **New**, and click **Folder**. (Rename the folder if you wish.)

5 Right-click the new folder and choose **Share** from the context menu.

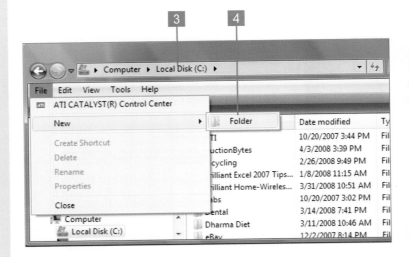

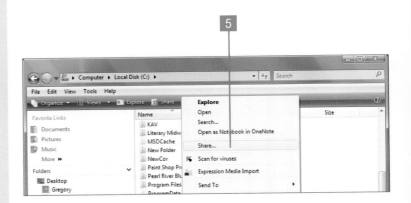

Setting up a shared folder (cont.)

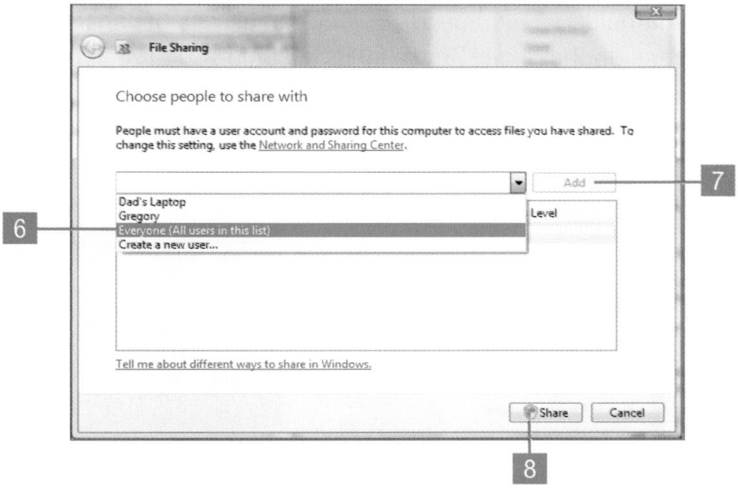

6. Choose **Everyone** from the drop-down list.
7. Click **Add**.
8. Click **Share**.
9. When a User Account Control dialogue box appears, click **Continue**.
10. On the next screen, click **Done**.

11

Did you know?

Who knew there were so many ways to share? You can also right-click a folder that already contains files you want to share and share it by choosing **Share** from the context menu. You can also set up file sharing by right-clicking a folder and choosing **Properties** from the context menu.

Creating user accounts and passwords

1. Click the **Start** button on the taskbar.
2. Click **Control Panel**.
3. Click **Add or remove user accounts**.

The good news is that, in the previous task, you shared a folder. The bad news is that you left it open to anyone on your network – as well as any hackers or 'wardrivers' who are able to infiltrate your network. It's far safer to protect shared folders, drives or files by making them available only to users with accounts and passwords. It's easy to do so, as long as you communicate the account names and passwords with the account holders beforehand, so they can access the shared locations on their own. These steps assume you have already created such passwords. First, create a user account – a set of information that identifies a user on the network.

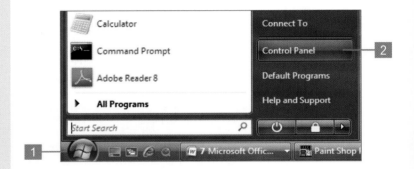

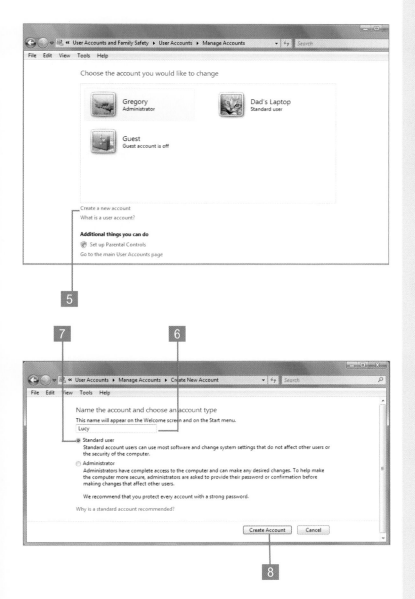

4 When a User Account Control dialogue box appears, click **Continue**.

5 Click **Create a new account**.

6 Type a name for the user.

7 Leave **Standard user** selected.

8 Click **Create Account**.

11

Creating user accounts and passwords (cont.)

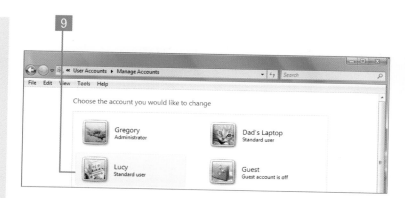

9 Click the name of the new account you just created.

10 When a User Account Control dialogue box appears, click **Continue**.

11 Click **Create a password**.

12 Type the password twice.

13 Type a password hint.

14 Click **Create password**.

Use this screen to change the picture associated with the user account.

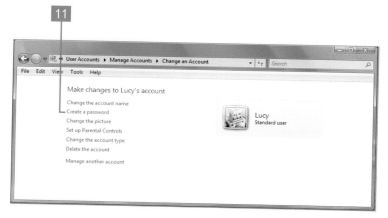

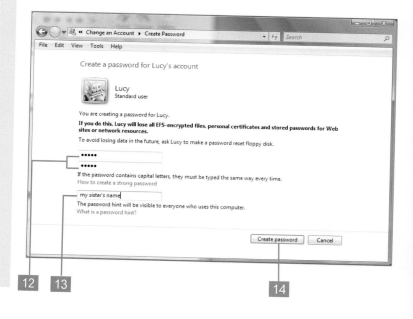

? Did you know?

When it comes to accounts, one is not always enough. You can have three types of account: standard, administrator and guest. Guest is for visitors; administrator gives you full create-and-delete privileges; standard lets you view and edit files, create files, and delete the files you created. After you create a password for another user, be sure to tell the user what the password is – or have the user select a password before you enter it.

Pros and cons of File and Print Sharing

You might well ask why you have the ability to turn File and Print Sharing on or off. Why wouldn't you want to share printers with other members of your household?

The big problem is that you might end up sharing a few resources other than printers with people who aren't either friends or family. In the past, File and Print Sharing was seen as a security risk. It was used (or rather, misused) by hackers who were able to gain access to internal networks using it. Once they gained access, they could grab your audio files or financial records.

The many firewalls provided by your router, your operating system and third-party security companies should prevent users outside your network from accessing such resources. But you need to make use of those firewalls: activate your built-in Windows firewall, and install a third-party firewall, using it as described earlier in this chapter.

11

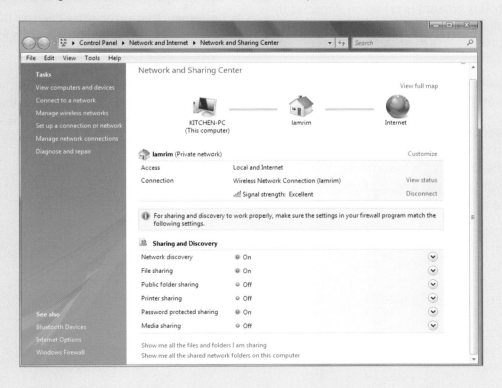

All about file permissions

When you share resources on your computer with other network users, you need to establish two things: who can access those resources and what they can do with them.

The question of who can access the resources is determined by the kind of account you allow. When you share a folder or other resource, you can grant access to three types of individuals or groups:

- **Guest**. This account is set up on Windows by default. It is intended for visitors who want temporary access to resources on your computer.

- **Everyone**. As the name implies, this option allows you to share a resource with anyone.

An individual user. In this case you specify a user who is required to enter a password to access the resource you are sharing. You can add as many users as you wish, but you need to add them one by one.

If you decide to specify individual users (which is the most secure choice), you can exercise some additional control by assigning each person a level of access. Each person can be assigned one of the following roles:

- **Reader**. The user can only view files (or read them) but not edit them.

- **Contributor**. The user can view files and add new ones. They have the ability to edit or delete only the files that they created originally.

- **Co-owner**. This option gives the user the ability to view, change, add or delete any file in the folder or drive being shared.

The co-owner option is the least secure, and you need to think long and hard about whether to grant this level of access. Personally, the whole idea makes me nervous.

Once you have set up a user account and protected it with a password, you can designate a password-protected resource. I know it's getting hard to keep track of all these passwords and what they do, but keep in mind that the password you created in the preceding task was only to enable the user to log on to your computer. If the user has an account on another computer on your network, you can enable that person to connect to a shared folder, drive or file and require that user to enter a password to access it.

1 Right-click the network connection icon in the system tray.

2 Choose **Network and Sharing Center**.

3 Click **Turn on file sharing** if necessary.

4 Click **Turn on password protected sharing** if necessary.

5 Click **Apply**.

6 When a User Account Control dialogue box appears, click **Continue**.

11

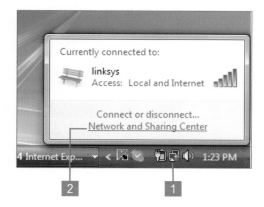

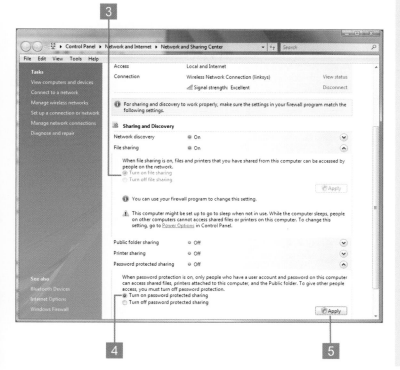

Sharing a password-protected resource (cont.)

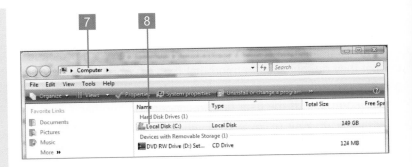

7 Click **Start** and click **Computer**.

8 Double-click your disk drive to open it.

9 Click **File**, click **New**, and click **Folder** to create a new folder.

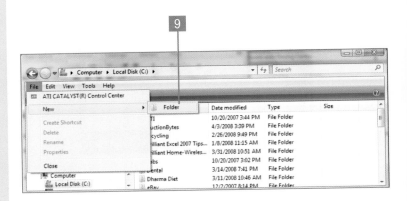

10 Type a new name for the folder and press Enter.

11 Right-click the new folder and choose **Share**.

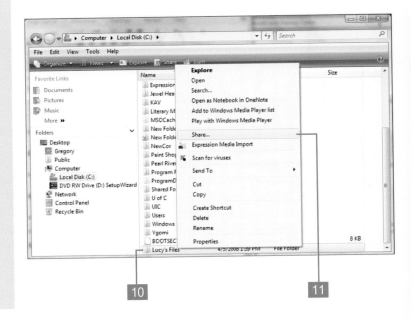

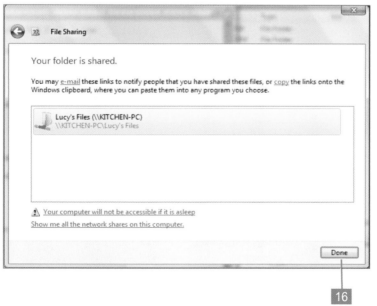

Sharing a password-protected resource (cont.)

12 Choose the name of the user from the drop-down list.

13 Click **Add**.

14 Click **Share**.

15 When a User Account Control dialogue box appears, click **Continue**.

16 Click **Done**.

11

? Did you know?

Just because someone has access doesn't mean they can pry into every nook and cranny. For extra security, you can hide a shared file. That way, when someone browses through the files on your computer, they won't be able to see it. This prevents them from directly connecting to the shared file as described later in this chapter. To hide a shared file, when you name the file simply add the £ sign after it. If the file is called share, for instance, name it share£.

Setting advanced sharing options

Once you have set up password protection for shared resources on your computer, any users who attempt to access a shared folder will be required to enter a password. You can adjust the level of permissions granted to each user or limit the number of users who can access the file simultaneously by sharing a folder or other resource as described in the preceding task and then following these steps.

1 Right-click the folder you just shared and choose **Properties**.

2 Click **Sharing**.

3 Click **Advanced Sharing**.

4 When a User Account Control dialogue box appears, click **Continue**.

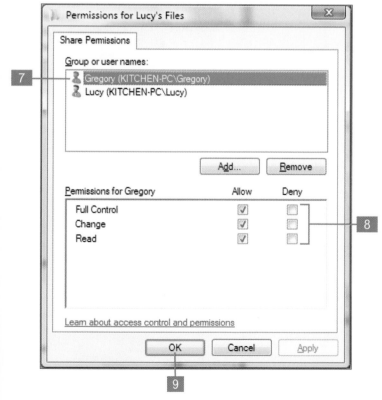

Setting advanced sharing options (cont.)

5 Adjust the number of simultaneous users who can access the file.

6 Click **Permissions**.

7 Click the user whose permissions you want to adjust.

8 Click **Deny** next to any permissions you want to deny for that user.

9 Click **OK**.

11

Adjusting how your computer stores shared resources

The term 'cache' may formerly have conjured up images of espionage and intrigue, but nowadays it accomplishes the opposite. A *cache* is a portion of your computer memory that is set aside for storing information that helps programs run more smoothly. In the case of shared files, caching allows users who access those files to store them in a cache area on their computer. Once the files are stored in the cache, those users can view the files even when they are offline – when they are travelling with their laptop and away from home, for instance.

1 Follow steps 1–4 in the preceding task to open the Advanced Sharing window.

2 Click **Share this folder** if necessary.

3 Click **Caching**.

4 Click one of the caching options:

A Click here to give the user control over what files to cache – they can choose only the ones that are needed while travelling.

B Click here to cache all shared files.

C Click here to prevent any files from being cached.

5 Click **OK**.

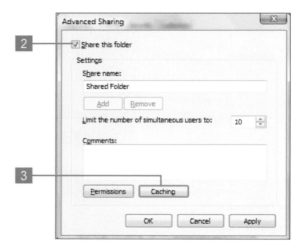

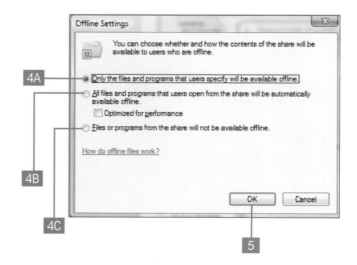

One thing about having a computer is that you always get lots of choices. For instance, the Advanced Sharing dialogue box contains a button labelled **Add**. This button allows you to add multiple sharing policies that can apply different standards to different sets of users. With multiple policies in place, you also have the opportunity to choose different sharing scenarios for different situations: you can choose one when your children or grandchildren are visiting, and another one when you have other guests staying with you, for instance.

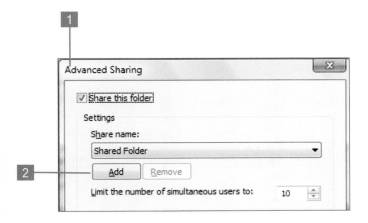

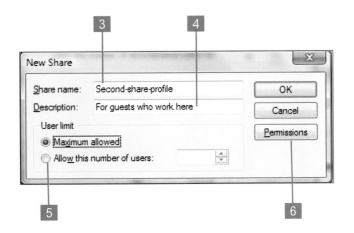

Assigning multiple sharing policies to the same resource

1. Open the Advanced Sharing window as described in the previous task.
2. Click **Add**.
3. Type a name for your new share setting.
4. Type a description so you know the purpose of the share.
5. Click here to limit the number of users.
6. Click **Permissions**.

11

Assigning multiple sharing policies to the same resource (cont.)

7 Click **Add** if you want to specify individual users.

8 Tick or untick permissions options.

9 Click **OK**.

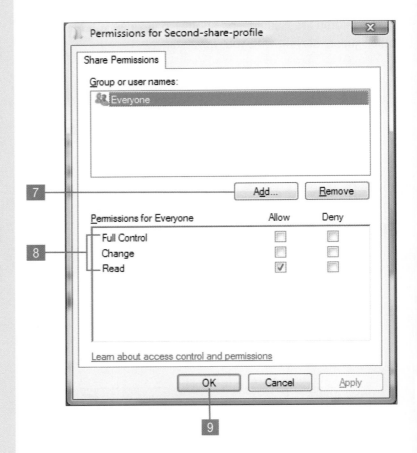

What we're talking about here is that what you see is what you get. Once all of your computers are networked, you can locate them by looking in the Network window. You can double-click them to view any shared contents. You can't view all of the files on the computer unless they have all been shared by the owner. You can view only the printers and other resources the owner has designated for sharing with others on the network.

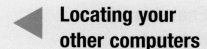

Locating your other computers

1 Click the **Start** button on the taskbar.

2 Click **Network**.

3 Double-click other networked computers to explore them.

4 Double-click networked resources to make use of them.

11

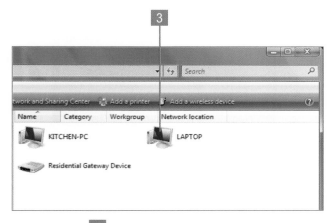

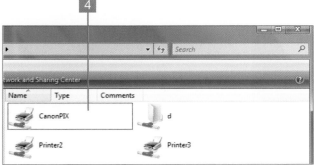

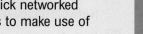

For your information

What happens when you know perfectly well that something is there, but you're being told that it doesn't exist? If you can't see other computers on your network and Network Discovery is active, make sure all of your network computers are on the same network. The network name needs to be spelled exactly the same on all machines.

Enabling Network Discovery

Nobody likes to be invisible. You need to make sure Network Discovery is turned on so your Windows Vista computer can be seen by other networked devices. If other computers on the network can't see your computer, follow these steps.

1. Right-click the network connection icon in the System Tray.

2. Click **Network and Sharing Center**.

3. Click the up arrow next to **Network discovery**.

4. Click **Turn on network discovery** if this option isn't selected already.

5. Click **Windows Firewall** if you cannot turn Network Discovery on or off.

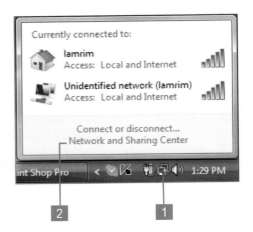

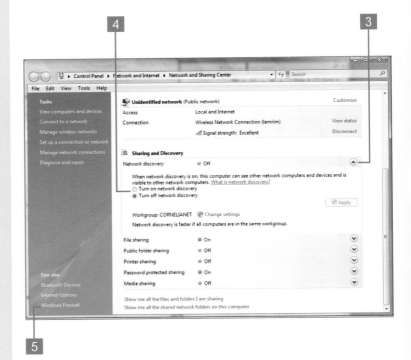

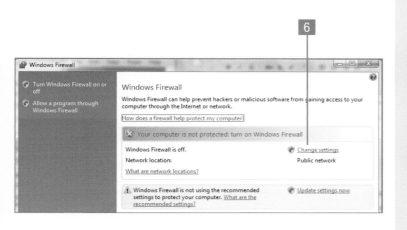

6 Click **Change settings**.

7 When a User Account Control dialogue box appears, click **Continue**.

8 Click **On**.

9 Click **OK**.

11

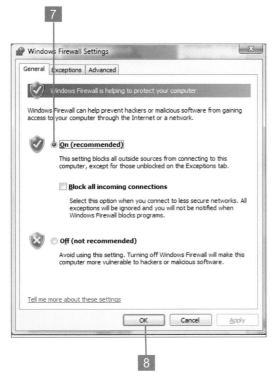

Directly accessing a shared resource on Windows XP

1. Click the **Start** button on the taskbar.
2. Click **All Programs**, **Accessories**, and then **Command Prompt**.

Okay, what if you're starting to get frustrated? Sometimes you can't see a computer on the network and troubleshooting proves difficult. This might occur if you have a 'mixed' network of computers running different operating systems (or different versions of the same system, such as Windows 95, Windows XP, Windows Vista and so on). If you know the IP address of the computer you want to access and the name of the shared folder on that computer, you can directly access the resource you want. A previous task explained how to view your IP address on your Windows Vista computer. The steps here show how to find the address on Windows XP.

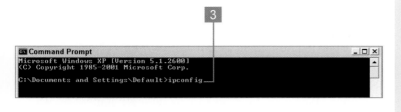

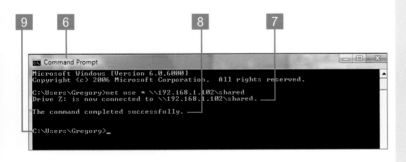

Directly accessing a shared resource on Windows XP (cont.)

3 Type **ipconfig** and then press **Enter**.

4 Write down the computer's IP address (in this example, 192.168.1.102).

5 Write down the names of any shared folders, which have a 'hand' icon holding their folder icon.

6 Return to your Windows Vista computer and open a command prompt window by clicking **Start**, typing **cmd**, and pressing **Enter**.

7 Type the following and click **Enter** (substitute the IP address and shared folder name on the computer you want to access): **Net use * \\192.168.1.102\shared**

8 Look for the response 'The command completed successfully', which means you have accessed the shared folder.

9 Type the name of the file you want to open and press **Enter**.

11

Sharing a network drive

1. Click **Start** and choose **Computer** to open the Computer window.

2. Right-click the drive you want to share and choose **Share** from the context menu.

3. Click **Advanced Sharing**.

4. When a User Account Control dialogue box appears, click **Continue**.

5. Click **Share this folder**.

We've been talking about passing around little pieces to taste, but it's also possible to share the entire pie. Previous tasks have explained how to share a folder on your network. You can also share an entire disk drive. You might need to do this if you need to access your own files from multiple locations, or if someone else needs to access many different folders on your file system. When you share a drive, it acquires a special name: network drive.

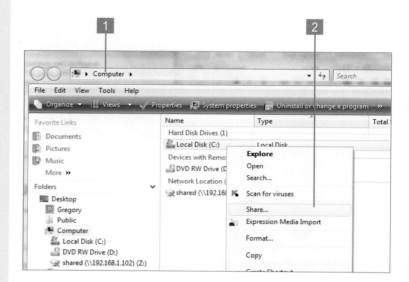

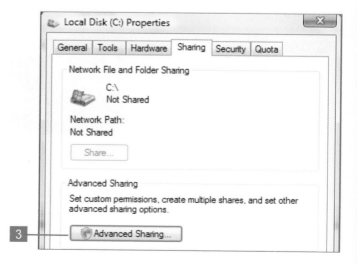

6 Change the share name if needed.

7 Click **Permissions**.

8 Tick the boxes next to the permissions you want to allow.

9 Click **Add**.

11

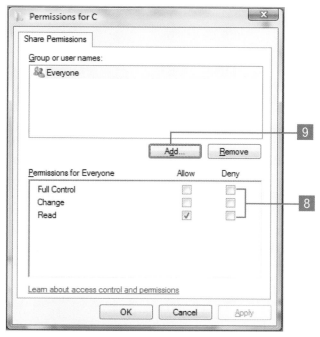

Sharing a network drive (cont.)

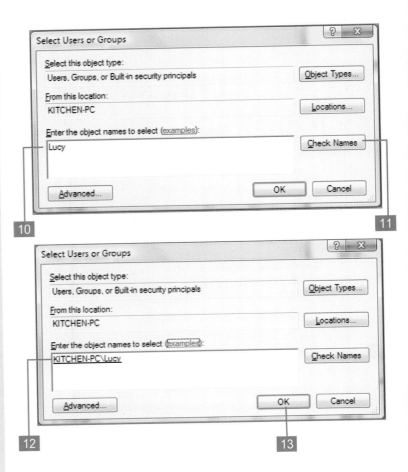

10 Type the name of the user to whom you want to grant access.

11 Click **Check Names**.

12 After the name changes, type any other names you want to add, and click **Check Names** after each one.

13 When you're done, click **OK**.

14 Click **OK** or **Close** to close any other open dialogue boxes.

For your information

Flash drives have alleviated the need to share entire disk drives. They make it easy to carry files from one place to another. But let's pause for a moment and consider the situation. It's possible that you could make a whole lot of files available. If you're thinking of giving someone access to your entire disk drive, first you should protect it with passwords. Second, ask yourself how much you really trust each and every potential user.

Communicating across the network

Introduction

Once you create a home network and have your computers talking to one another, you gain the ability to solve a variety of technical problems. If you only have one printer in your home, for instance, can you use it to print from all the available computers you have networked? Can you configure your network so your niece can play a game in one room and your grandson can play in another room on a different computer?

In each case, the answer is yes. Home networking isn't just about sharing files stored on computers. It's also about getting your digital devices to talk to one another. In this chapter, you'll learn about different ways to use your network to do printing and gaming, and to perform other functions.

What you'll do

Share a printer

Verify a shared printer's name

Add a shared printer

Print remote files on your local printer

Get the hardware you need for network gaming

Use a wireless gaming adapter

Sharing a printer

1. Make sure your printer is equipped with a print server. A server can be:
   - a specially designated hardware device such as the JP JetDirect EW2400, which works with many different models of HP printers
   - an external or internal server specially made for your printer by its manufacturer.

2. Click the **Start** button on the taskbar.

3. Choose **Control Panel**.

4. Click **Printer**.

You might have a computer in every room in your home, but that doesn't mean you need multiple printers. Just as your networked computers can share an Internet connection and share files, they can share access to other hardware devices. You don't have to have a wireless network in place, either.

Once you have a home network (either wired or wireless), one of the big benefits is the ability to share printers. You can still have more than one printer – a high-quality laser printer can be used for photos, and a less expensive inkjet one can be used for text files. But the point is that all of your computers can have access to any one of them. You just need to make sure the printers you use are compatible with home networking, something you can check with each printer's documentation.

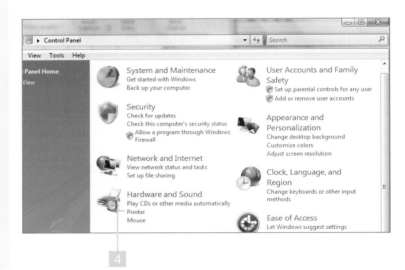

Sharing a printer (cont.)

5 Right-click the printer you want to share and choose **Sharing** from the context menu.

6 Click **Change sharing options**.

7 When a User Account Control dialogue box appears, click **Continue**.

12

Communicating across the network 193

Sharing a printer (cont.)

8 When the properties dialogue box for the printer reappears, click **Share this printer**.

9 If necessary, assign the shared printer a name.

10 Click **OK**.

If the printer you want to share is connected to another computer (such as a machine running Windows XP), you can access it as long as your computer and the one that is connected to the printer are both on the network. First, you need to verify the name of the printer.

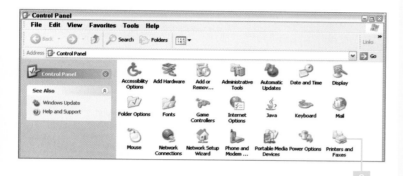

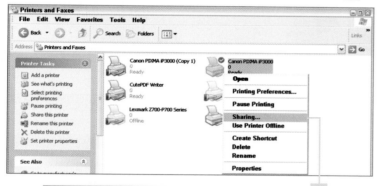

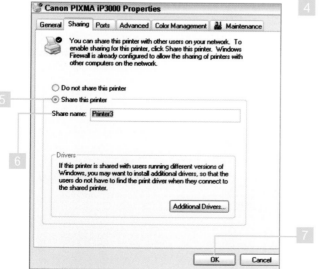

Verifying a shared printer's name

1. Click **Start**.

2. Choose **Control Panel**.

3. Double-cick **Printers and Faxes**.

4. Right-click the printer you want to share and choose **Sharing** from the context menu.

5. Click **Share this printer**

6. Give the printer a name, if necessary, and make a note of the name.

7. Click **OK**.

12

Adding a shared printer

Once you have shared a printer on another computer and verified its name, you need to connect to that printer. You might have to install a driver for the shared printer, but Windows Vista can do that for you.

1 Switch to your own computer and click the **Start** button on the taskbar.

2 Choose **Control Panel**.

3 Add the shared printer

4 Click **Printer**.

5 Double-click **Add Printer**.

6 Click **Add a network, wireless or Bluetooth printer**.

7 Click **Next**.

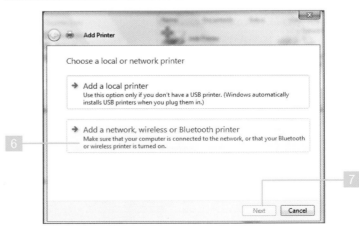

Adding a shared printer (cont.)

8. Click the name of the printer you want to share.

9. Click **Next**.

10. Click **Install driver**.

11. When a User Account Control dialogue box appears, click **Continue**.

12. Verify the printer name.

13. Tick here to make this the default printer.

14. Click **Next**.

12

Adding a shared printer (cont.)

15 Click here to print a test page.

16 Click **Finish**.

17 Once the printer driver is installed and you are connected to the shared printer, you can choose it from the drop-down list at the top of the Print dialogue box.

18 Click **OK** to print on the remote printer.

For your information

Before you can print across the network, you need to make sure you have File and Print Sharing enabled.

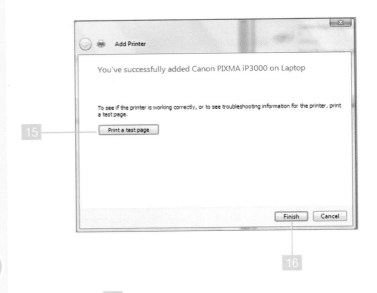

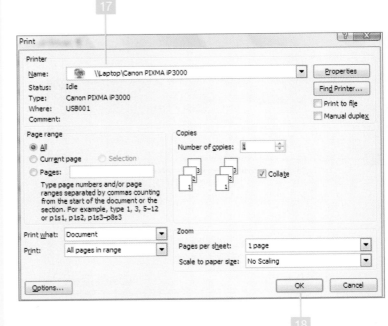

Suppose you have files you need to print, but they aren't contained on the file system of the computer you're using; they're on a computer in another part of the house. Because you are networked, you can use the nearest printer in your home to print documents that are on any computer in your home. In order to do so, you first need to set up a remote desktop connection. You only need to establish such a connection once; the connections are saved so you don't have to recreate them the next time you connect.

Printing remote files on your local printer

1 Click the **Start** button on the taskbar.

2 Type **remote desktop connection**.

3 When the Remote Desktop Connection application appears, press **Enter**.

4 Click **Options**.

5 Click the **Local Resources** tab.

6 Check **Printers**.

7 Click **Connect**.

Gaming across your network: get the hardware you need

Other hardware needs: Ethernet

1 Purchase a router with multiple ports.

2 Connect your gaming devices to the router with Ethernet cable.

A home network is idea for allowing multiple players to play the same game from different locations. There are two problems that commonly arise, however: the Ethernet and other cables needed to connect the players to the game console and the network can be unwieldy, and performance lags can make gaming virtually impossible.

For Nintendo®

Purchase a Nintendo GameCube™ broadband adapter.

For Sony Playstation®

Purchase a Sony Playstation broadband adapter.

For Microsoft® Xbox 360™

Since the Xbox is already connected to your broadband modem, you don't need to purchase an adapter.

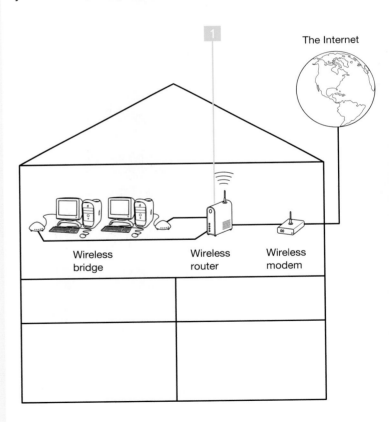

The Internet

Wireless bridge

Wireless router

Wireless modem

Gaming across your network: get the hardware you need (cont.)

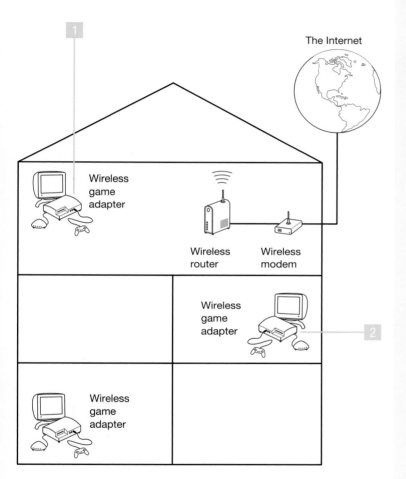

The Internet

Wireless game adapter

Wireless router

Wireless modem

Wireless game adapter

Wireless game adapter

Other hardware needs: wireless

1. Purchase a wireless router with multiple ports.

2. Connect wireless Ethernet bridges to each of your game consoles so they can communicate with the wireless router and with each other.

12

Using a wireless gaming adapter

A special type of hardware called a wireless gaming adapter is designed to form a bridge between a wireless router and your game consoles. One advantage of such a device is that you need virtually no Ethernet cable to get your games up and running. Another is that you have an integrated solution: as long as you have your game consoles and a wireless modem ready, you can purchase all the hardware you need in a single package.

1. Purchase a device like the Netgear WGE111 wireless gaming adapter.

2. Connect the Netgear device to one of your gaming consoles. Turn on the adapter and let it automatically detect your network.

3. If you have a second gaming console and want to network it to the first one, purchase a second wireless gaming adapter and attach it.

Did you know?

If you purchase two wireless game adapters, such as the Netgear WGE111, they can connect to one another directly in an ad-hoc network; you don't need to be connected to a router or to the Internet. Many such adapters conxtain a switch that allows you to move between ad-hoc networks and conventional wireless Internet connections.

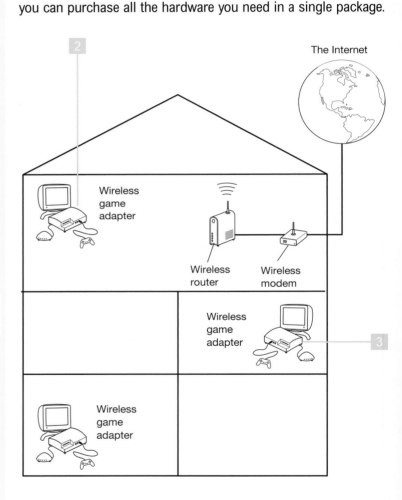

The Internet

Wireless game adapter

Wireless router   Wireless modem

Wireless game adapter

Wireless game adapter

Networking a game console

I hear what you're saying: 'At my age, I'm not going to start playing computer games.' I have news for you: when you see the variety of games that are available and what you can do with them, you might reconsider how you spend your leisure time. People over 50 all over the world are enjoying game systems like the Nintendo Wii that can lead them through exercise routines or do 'virtual bowling' or 'virtual tennis'.

If you don't believe me, just review the stories in your local media. For instance, you'll find an article in the *Guardian* entitled 'Nintendo's Wii Captures New Game Market' at **http://www.guardian.co.uk/business/2007/oct/10/usnews.internationalnews**.

You don't need a network to run a game system like the Wii. You don't even need a computer, for that matter. A system like the Wii, the Microsoft Xbox or the Sony Playstation comes with a controller called a game console. The console is what plays the game and contains the controls you need to participate. But if you do have a network, you have more flexibility about where and how you can use the system. You can play online games from any location in your house, and you can play games from two different locations, for instance.

In order to add a game console to your home Ethernet network, you simply obtain an Ethernet cable and plug it into the router as you would one of your computers. The computer that assigns IP addresses dynamically to each of your network devices using DHCP automatically assigns the device an address.

To connect a console to your wireless network, you have a few more things to consider. First, you need to know the SSID and any network passwords you have specified (see Chapter 8 for more on SSIDs; see Chapter 10 for more on network passwords). Once you have this information at hand, follow these steps:

1. Obtain a wireless adapter that is specifically designed for the game console you have purchased.
2. Use an Ethernet cable to connect the adapter to your wireless router.
3. Turn on your adapter, and then turn on your game console.
4. Insert the setup disk that came with the wireless adapter you purchased for your game console.
5. Follow the steps in the setup wizard; they include entering the network SSID and passwords as well as the security protocol you are using (WEP, for instance).

Once you complete the setup routine your wireless router should locate your game console wirelessly so you can start using it on the network. The adapter you have purchased for your game console is connected to the router using Ethernet; the game consoles work wirelessly so they can be moved around freely.

12

If you can't connect to the network or other computers

Introduction

The goal of the chapters you've read so far has been to make it easier for you to connect your computers to each other and to the Internet. Despite following all the steps, however, you might still run into connection problems. Don't worry: it happens to the best of us. In fact trouble often starts to brew because of conditions that are not under your control, such as the level of network traffic or problems with your ISP.

It's frustrating to shop for all the hardware you need, hook it up just right and have everything working smoothly, only to run into connection problems at some point. The most basic network problem usually has to do with the quality of the cables or the wireless signal. But other problems can be solved by following simple exercises. Spending just a few minutes to check connections can help save time and service calls in the long run.

What you'll do

Check the status of your network
Gather the data you need from your ISP
Identify your network card's physical address
Install and configure your wireless router
Automatically configure your router/access point
Change your router's password
Change your IP address information
Relocate your wireless router
Understand problems with shared DSL connections
Check inconsistent network connections
Change your wireless channel
Adjust your wireless antenna
Purchase a new wireless antenna
Add a network repeater
Clear interference from cordless phones
Avoid interference from other home appliances
Track down interference from other networking equipment
Track problems outside your home
Track other environmental issues
Trace firewall problems
Check for spyware and viruses
Check why your network adapter won't connect
Disable firewalls when networking printers

Checking your Internet connection

Let's say that you wake up one bright, sunny day ready to use your computer. But you can't connect to your network at all. It's logical just to keep on checking your network connections until you find the one that is broken. Whether you have a wired or wireless network, you need to find the component that's not working. Be systematic and start from the point where your Internet connection comes into your house, and you'll find the problem. In most cases, it will be simple to repair.

1 Check your broadband modem and make sure the DSL or cable light is solidly on and not blinking.

2 If the light is not on or is blinking, call your ISP to report the problem.

3 Check your home router or hub and make sure the Internet light is on. If it is not, turn the router off and on to reset it.

4 Make sure all the connectors are seated firmly in the ports.

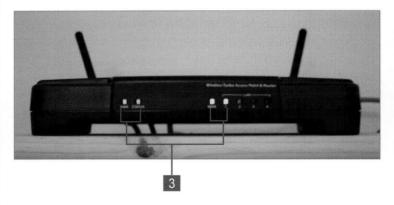

Did you know?

The tab on the end of a CAT-5 cable holds it in place in the Ethernet port. If the tab breaks out, the connector can easily slip loose. The cable looks as if it is connected, but the connection is actually broken. Push the cable in firmly. Then consider taping it in place to keep it from slipping out again.

If you follow the steps presented in the preceding task and discover that your Internet connection is functioning properly and other computers can get online, your computer is your next likely suspect. The most obvious place to check is your Ethernet cable (if you have a wired network connection). If that is functioning properly, try the troubleshooting steps presented below.

 ## Checking your computer hardware

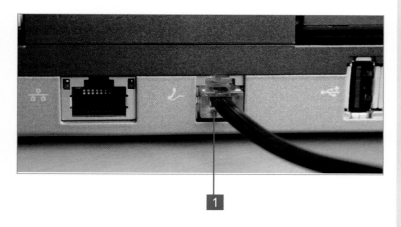

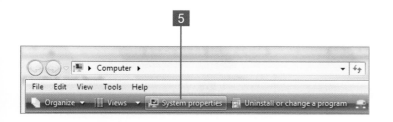

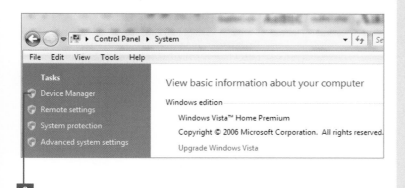

Check your cable

1 Make sure your cable is plugged securely to your computer's Ethernet port.

2 If the cable is plugged in but you still don't have a connection, make sure your cable is working (replace the cable).

13

Check your card

3 Click the **Start** button on the taskbar.

4 Choose **Computer**.

5 Click **System properties**.

6 Click **Device Manager**.

7 When a User Account Control dialogue box appears, click **Continue**.

Checking your computer hardware (cont.)

8 Click the plus sign next to Network adapters.

9 Double-click the card you want to check.

10 Make sure you see the message 'This device is working properly'.

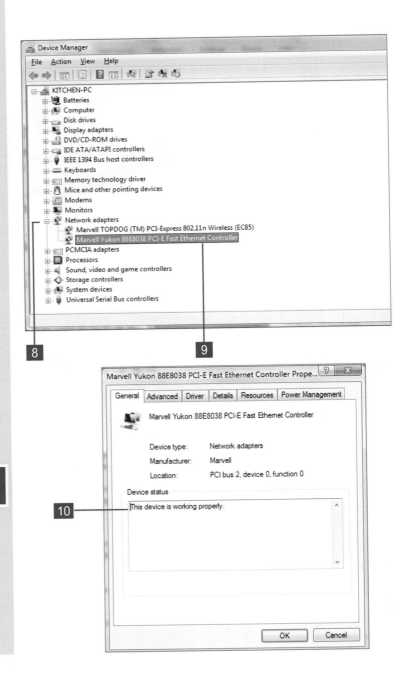

? **Did you know?**

If you see a message indicating that your network card is malfunctioning, you may need to update its driver. Click the **Driver** tab and click the **Update Driver** button.

Your network card and cable connections are only one type of check you can perform on your network connection. If the hardware is working properly, the problem might be software-related. Some simple diagnostics should help to identify the problem and get you reconnected. I have found that, if available memory is running very low, the system lacks the resources needed to establish a connection. Freeing up more memory and/or restarting the computer sometimes helps to get the connection up and running again.

Checking your computer software

Check your memory

1 Right-click the disk drive you want to use and choose **Properties**.

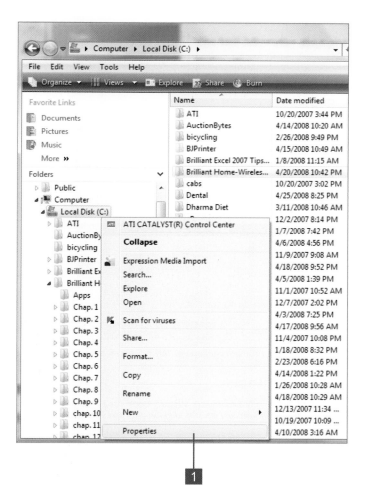

1

13

Checking your computer software (cont.)

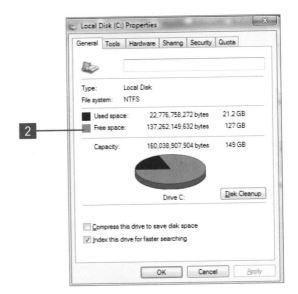

2 Check your available memory.

Use Diagnose and repair

1 Click the network connection icon in the System Tray.

2 Click **Diagnose and repair**.

3 After the diagnostic tool is complete, click the solution that applies to you.

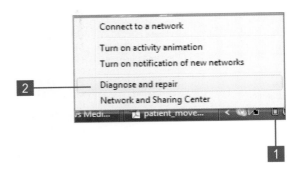

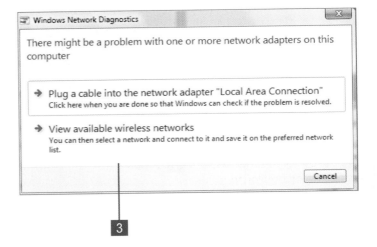

If you try the simple network checks described to this point and you still can't get online or connected to other computers, you might want to call your Internet Service Provider (ISP) for help.

When you discuss your intermittent or broken network connection with your ISP, the technical support staff might lead you through a process called Release and Renew. This is a process you can do on your own, too. When you establish a connection to the Internet, your computer obtains a 'lease' to go online. By releasing the connection and then renewing it, you might find that any unnecessary information that's keeping you from going online is 'flushed' out and your connection works once again.

Renewing and releasing your connection

1. Click the **Start** button on the taskbar.

2. Type **cmd** and press **Enter** to open a command prompt

13

For your information

The Release and Renew commands described here require you to be logged into the computer with administrator privileges.

Renewing and releasing your connection (cont.)

③ Type **ipconfig /release** (be sure to type a single space before the forward-slash (/) and then press **Enter**.

④ When the message appears listing the IP address as blank or 0.0.0.0 and the next command prompt appears, type **ipconfig /renew** and press **Enter**. window.

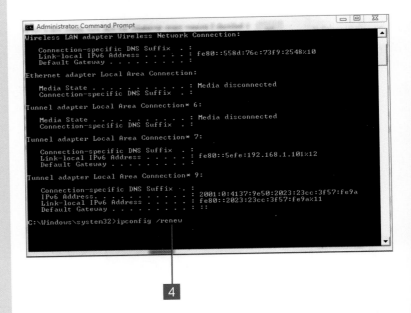

Did you know?

The **ipconfig** command has a number of other functions besides release and renew. Type **ipconfig /?** and press **Enter** to view them. You'll see a list that includes such commands as **ipconfig /all**, which displays your full Internet connection information, for instance.

The tasks up to this point can be applied to all kinds of home networks. But if you use Powerline products, you might want to try some troubleshooting approaches specific to them. Powerline products are supposed to allow home networking products to connect to the network and one another wirelessly. But if they don't allow you to connect, there are a number of simple steps you can follow to troubleshoot them.

◀ **Checking your Powerline connection**

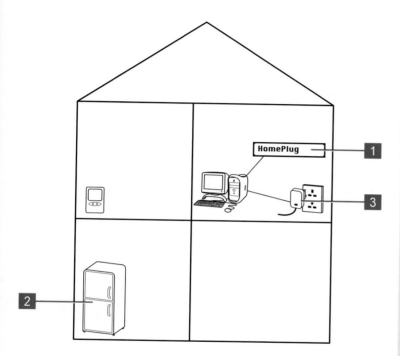

1 Check your password. Make sure the same network password is used with all the Powerline devices.

2 Turn off any appliances that may be drawing a large amount of electrical power such as microwaves or hair dryers.

3 Reset your Powerline adapter according to your manufacturer's instructions.

13

For your information

Although it seems like a surge protector should be a good thing to use, you should always plug your Powerline connection into a wall socket instead of a surge protector. Surge protectors don't work properly with Powerline network adaptors because the surge protection technology interrupts the flow of data. Most Powerline adapters have surge protection built in. This means that, if the power to the mains surges suddenly, the device will shut off without being damaged.

Checking Link Layer Topology Discovery Mapper

▶

Suppose you've checked all of your hardware, and your ISP says your network connection is working fine. If you still can't connect to other computers on your home network, the problem might have to do with your software rather than hardware connections.

Remember playing hide-and-seek when you were a kid? Now your computer may be hiding from others on your network. One of the most common networking problems is the inability to 'see' other computers on your network. A number of problems might cause computers to be undiscoverable (for instance, network names that are different on different computers). The place to start, though, is with the most basic problem: the protocol (in other words, a set of instructions) that enables computers to be 'found' on the network, Link Layer Topology Discovery (LLTD), is disabled. To enable it, follow these steps.

1 Click the **Start** button on the taskbar.

2 Choose **Control Panel**.

3 Click **View network status and tasks**.

4 Click **Manage network connections**.

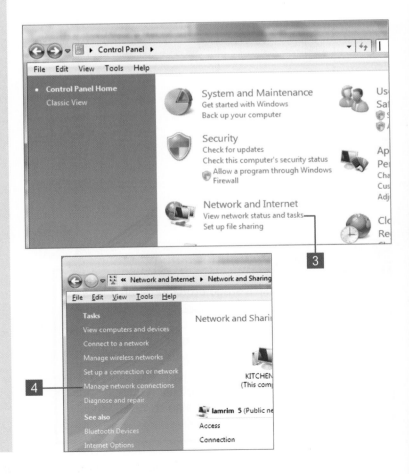

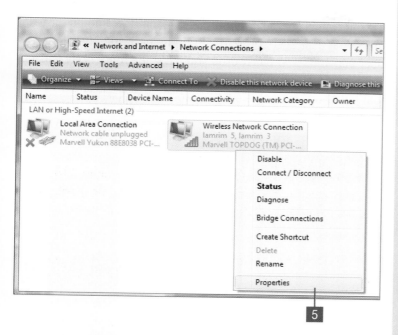

5 Right-click the network connection and choose **Properties**.

6 When a User Account Control dialogue box appears, click **Continue**.

7 Tick the box next to **Link Layer Topology Discovery Mapper I/O Driver**.

8 Check the box next to **Link Layer Topology Discovery Responder**.

9 Click **OK**.

13

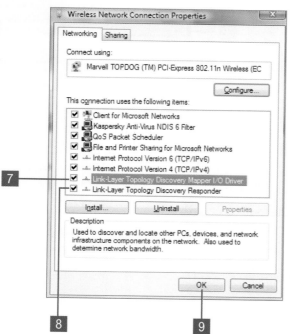

If you can't connect to the network or other computers 215

Creating a password reset disk

1. Click the **Start** button on the taskbar.

2. Type **user accounts**.

3. When User Accounts appears, press **Enter**.

4. Connect a USB flash drive to your computer, or insert a CD in the CD-ROM drive.

5. Click **Create a password reset disk**.

If you're like me, you spend more time than you'd like to admit looking for your glasses and keys. Keeping track of a lot of passwords is sometimes too much to ask. When you create a home network, you might have access to multiple computers in your home. For security purposes, each user should have an individual user account to log on to the network. The more user accounts and passwords you have, the more likely you'll forget or lose one of those passwords. One way to recover a lost password is to create a password reset disk.

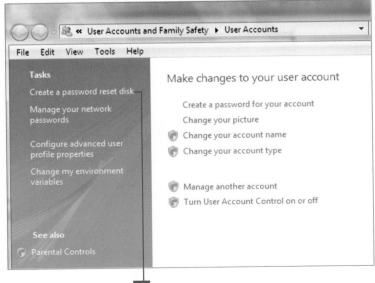

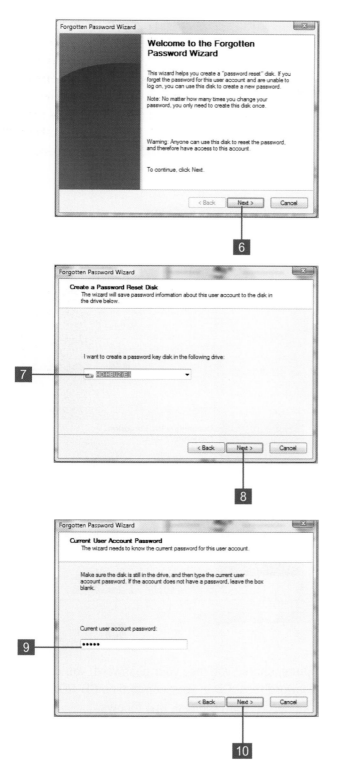

Creating a password reset disk (cont.)

6. Click **Next**.

7. If necessary, choose the drive where you will save your password information.

8. Click **Next**.

9. Type your current user account password.

10. Click **Next**.

If you can't connect to the network or other computers 217

Creating a
password reset
disk (cont.)

11 When progress is complete, click **Next**.

12 Click **Finish**.

13 Label and save your CD (if you used one).

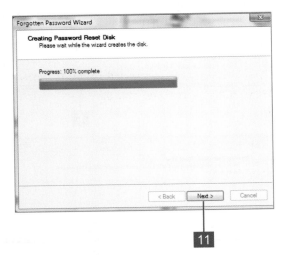

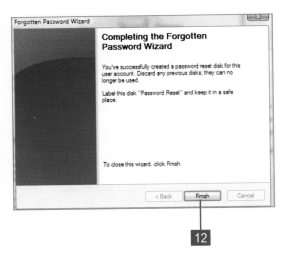

In the future, should you lose your password, you can insert your password reset CD in your computer's CD-ROM drive and reset it as described in the task that follows.

Network passwords, like other computer- and Internet-related passwords, are tricky. You have to remember them and in many cases they are case-sensitive. Yet, writing them down is risky because an unauthorised user might find them. If you don't write them down and store them in a secure location, however, you can easily forget your passwords. If you enter a password to access a shared folder or other network resource and the password doesn't work, you'll have to go to the owner and get the password reset.

If you have created a password reset disk as described in the preceding task, recovery is easy. You only need to follow these steps.

Retrieving a lost user account password

1 Attempt to log on to your account.

2 When the alert message appears, click **OK**.

13

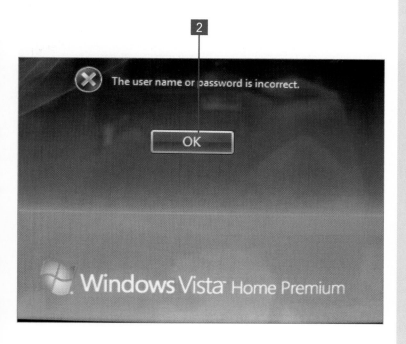

3 Click **Reset password**.

4 Insert your password reset disk and follow the steps in the Password Reset Wizard to restore your password.

Lucy

Password

Password Hint: my sister's name
Reset password...

3

For your information

Should you have Windows 'store' your wireless and other passwords so you don't have to log on every time you want to access a network resource? In a household where computers are shared by many members, including inquisitive and clever grandkids, it may not be a good idea. For sensitive passwords like those for your financial accounts, you should write them down. Then put the piece of paper in a place where others aren't likely to see it (but not so remote that you'll forget it yourself). Don't depend on Windows to save your passwords for you.

It's sad but true that things are likely to go wrong at the worst possible moment. Let's say that you really need to find something online. Your computer seems to be connected to the Internet, but you are unable to browse websites. Although your computer is connected, in other words, your browser can't establish a 'socket' connection that lets a browser surf websites. If that's the case, stopping and then resuming the network connection may establish the connection you need.

 Restarting your network connection

1 Click the **Start** button on the taskbar.

2 Choose **Network**.

3 Click **Network and Sharing Center**.

4 Click **View status**.

5 Click **Disable**.

13

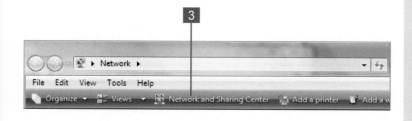

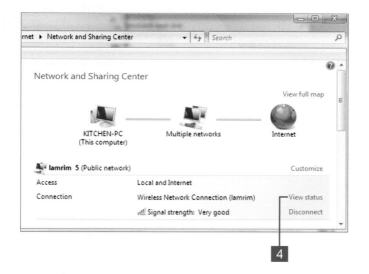

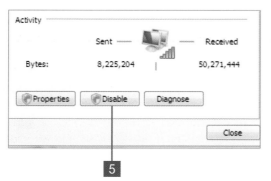

Restarting your network connection (cont.)

6 When a User Account Control box appears, click **Continue**.

7 When the connection is broken, click **Connect to a network**.

8 Follow the steps on the connection screen to connect to your network.

9 Click **Connect**.

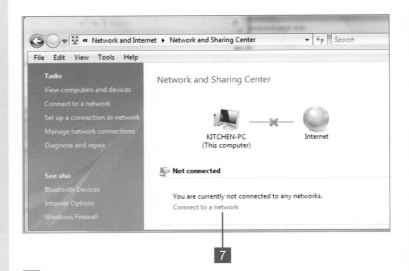

If you attempt to connect to your wireless network at home and you see a message stating that Windows cannot locate any networks, don't panic. You can try checking your broadband Internet connection and your router. Or you can try re-enabling your wireless network adapter.

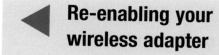

Re-enabling your wireless adapter

1 Click **Diagnose why Windows can't find any networks**.

2 Click **Enable the network adapter "Wireless Network Connection"** (your adapter name may differ).

13

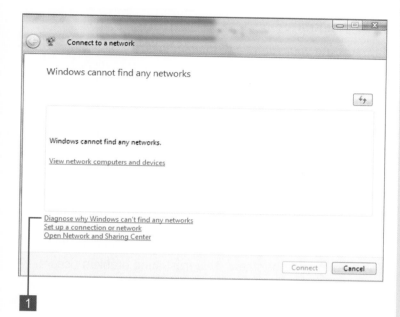

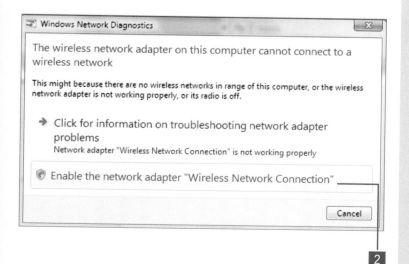

Recycling your router and modem

When all else fails and you are unable to connect to the Internet through network diagnostics or other software functions, you can turn to a hardware solution. Recycle your router and modem to reset your home's connection to the Internet.

1 Turn off your broadband router and your modem. (If you don't have on/off switches on these devices, unplug them from the mains.)

2 Wait 20 seconds.

3 Plug in the modem.

4 When the lights on the modem are on and no longer blinking, plug in the router.

5 When the LAN or WLAN light is on solidly and no longer blinking, check the Internet connection once again, and reconnect if necessary.

Did you know?

If recycling your router and modem fails, try restarting your computer. I know I've been telling you to restart a lot, but there's a reason for that. In this case, a lack of available resources and memory can prevent your computer from connecting to the Internet or performing other memory-intensive functions such as viewing movies or listening to streaming audio.

Inability to connect to the Internet or to other computers on your home network is only one type of network problem. Another problem that's just as common occurs when your network connections are intermittent — you can connect at some times and not others. This frustrating problem occurs most often with wireless networks, though a loose or damaged Ethernet cable can also cause intermittency in Ethernet networks.

Relocating your wireless router

A caveman would not have had a computer, but in some ways his habitat would have been better suited for networks than your house, which probably wasn't constructed with wireless communications in mind. The structures that make up most modern homes – walls, floors, roofs, doorways and windows – can have a dramatic effect on the quality of wireless communications. And I'm talking drama in the sense of tragedy, not comedy. Unfortunately, the first time you learn this is usually when you can't establish a reliable wireless connection from one of your computers to the Internet or other computers in your home.

If, however, you can do some advance planning, you can take some steps to ensure that your router is positioned optimally. That way, you'll avoid some of the barriers (pun intended) to network communications.

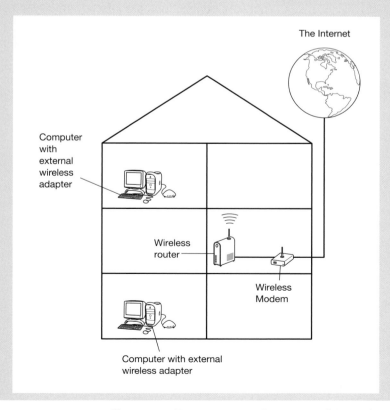

The Internet

Computer with external wireless adapter

Wireless router

Wireless Modem

Computer with external wireless adapter

Relocating your wireless router (cont.)

One good general rule of thumb is to place the router in a central location in your house – on the middle floor of the house, and in a location near the centre of the house rather than an outside wall. This makes it more likely that the wireless signal will be able to reach to all rooms in the home.

But suppose the centre of the home is not suitable, especially if it is the place where your refrigerator, central heating system, microwave, etc. are located. Placing the router very close to

electrical devices will degrade the signal and wreak havoc on your network communications. The best location is near your network computers, and away from potential interference.

For some special situations, a router with a long-range capability is preferable. But don't take the claims too seriously. Homes with lots of structural obstacles can still degrade the signal. You may be better off purchasing an upgraded antenna, a second access point or a repeater to boost the signal in your home.

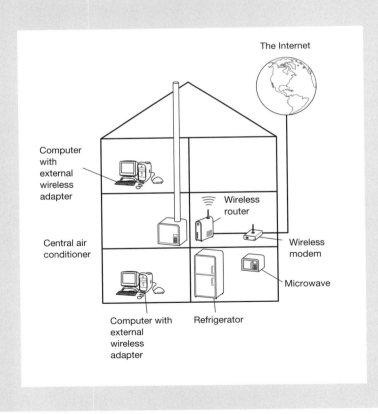

Problems with DSL and cable connections

You usually think that an urban area has technological advantages over more remote locations. But there are disadvantages to being around lots of other people who want to tune in and turn on. Cable modem technology is a cost-effective option for providing high-speed Internet connections over conventional cable television lines. But when users learn that their cable connection is actually one that they share with other residents in their neighbourhood, they are usually surprised.

The fact is that cable connections are distributed to subscribers in a particular area by means of a common connection. The quality of the connection experienced by any individual subscriber is affected by how much load the other customers on the same circuit are placing on the system. If dozens of subscribers are downloading movies or performing other bandwidth-intensive tasks at the same time, your own connection speed will suffer. If you live in a metropolitan area with lots of cable subscribers, you might get slower speeds than rural users.

With DSL, you don't have the problem of shared bandwidth, but you have a different situation. The DSL Internet connection is distributed to individual households over conventional copper telephone lines after passing through a connection point called a central office (CO). Your distance from the CO can affect the speed of your Internet connection.

In either case, if you experience speeds that are significantly slower than those advertised by your Internet Service Provider (ISP), or that fluctuate depending on the time of day, contact your provider. If you have cable, ask how many subscribers share your connection, and whether the load on the system is particularly heavy because of what your neighbours are doing online. If you have DSL, ask about your distance from the CO, and see if there is any way you can be moved to a closer circuit.

13

For your information

If you are having problems with inconsistent or on-again/off-again connections, see **http://www.security skeptic.com/homeplugnetworking.htm**

Changing wireless channels

▶

Your wireless connection to the Internet is divided into a range of frequencies. Each frequency is referred to as a channel. By 'changing the channel' (much as you would on a television) you might get some improvement on an intermittent connection. Your connection will work best if your router and network adapters all use the same channel for wireless communications.

1 In your browser's Address box, type the address of your router, 192.168.1.1, and press **Enter**.

2 Enter your administrative username and password and click **OK**.

3 When the router setup screen appears, click **Wireless**.

4 Choose a channel from the Wireless Channel drop-down list.

5 Click **Save Settings**.

For your information

In my experience, changing the wireless channel doesn't provide an instant solution. It can help, however, if you are experiencing interference from another wireless device such as a cordless phone that uses the same frequency range as your wireless router.

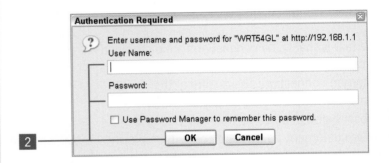

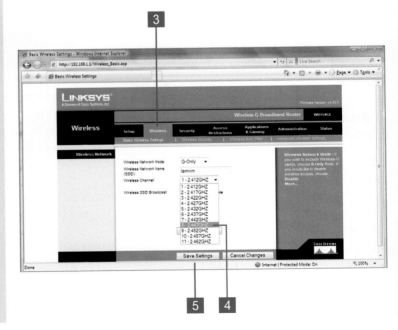

The typical, economical wireless home router has one or two antennas that transmit omni-directionally – in other words, the signal radiates out in all directions. Because the signal goes in all directions, it quickly loses strength with distance, especially when it runs into obstructions. Purchasing a second wireless antenna can help because it can be aimed in the direction of the computers or other devices with which it needs to communicate.

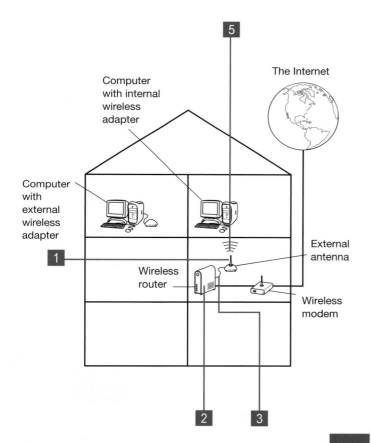

See also

Another solution to a home whose design presents obstructions to a wireless signal is the Home Power or Phoneline option.

◀ Buying a new antenna

1 Go to a site such as **http://www.amazon.co.uk**, where you can purchase a wireless antenna or Blue Unplugged (**http://www.blueunplugged.com/c.aspx?c=41122**), where you can find a Buffalo AirStation.

2 Make sure the protocol used is compatible with that of your router: if your router uses 802.11g, get an 802.11g antenna.

3 Make sure the cable that comes with the antenna and plugs into your router is long enough to let you position the antenna freely (some cables are short).

4 You may have to remove your router's existing antennas – make sure your router has detachable antennas beforehand.

5 Experiment with positioning the antenna until you get the desired results: your Internet connection is strong and steady.

13

Adding an access point

Large companies typically get far stronger wireless service than the average home. That's not because the structures in which the businesses are located have fewer sources of interference. It's because bigger enterprises are able to invest in site surveys and better equipment than the average homeowner can afford. You can do one thing the companies with 'deep pockets' can do, however: you can dramatically improve your wireless coverage by adding one or more access points to your home network.

1 Purchase a second router or access point; consider getting the same model or brand as your primary one so you can be sure they will work together.

2 Connect the secondary access point to one of your computers first before connecting it to the primary access point so you can configure it. Disconnect your other access point from that computer.

3 Log into the secondary access point from the computer to which it is connected by entering the default IP address, 192.168.1.1, in your web browser's address box and pressing **Enter**.

4 Enter the access point's username and password so you can administer it, and click **OK**.

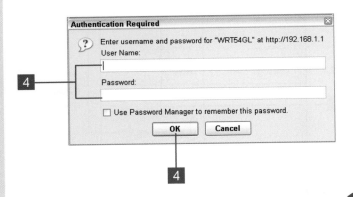

For your information

Adding an access point can be expensive. Not only do you have to purchase a second router/access point, but you have to buy the Ethernet cable to connect the primary access point to the secondary one. Chances are you want your secondary access point to be in a different room (or, more likely, a different floor) from the first one so you can extend the network range effectively. This means fishing Ethernet cable through the walls of your house and purchasing enough cable to reach the desired distance. You can use Home Power adapters to connect the routers, but these are expensive as well. A second antenna is a more cost-effective option and is simpler to install.

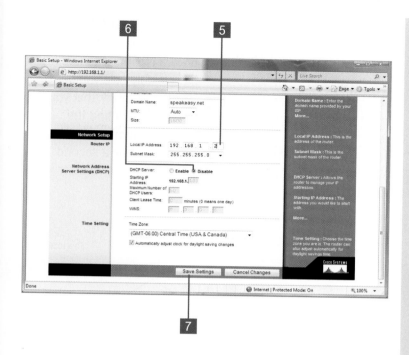

Adding an access point (cont.)

5 Scroll down to the area of the basic setup tab where the IP address for the access point is listed and change it to 192.168.1.2.

6 Disable DHCP.

7 Click **Save Settings**.

8 Click **Wireless**.

9 Click **Wireless Security**

10 Create a second security key if you want this access point's key to be different from the one on the primary access point (this is optional).

11 Click **Save Settings**.

12 Connect your secondary access point to your primary one with a length of Ethernet cable.

13

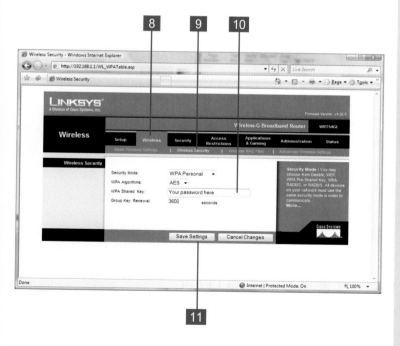

Adding a repeater

A repeater is a hardware device specially designed to function as a relay station for Wi-Fi signals within a home or business. Adding a repeater to your home network is similar to adding a second access point. A repeater will probably give you better performance; however, if you have a second router that you aren't using or can find one second-hand, you'll find the second access point option to be more economical. But if you have a large space to cover and you need to buy a second piece of hardware to relay your wireless signal, a repeater is your best option.

1 Purchase a repeater such as the Linksys WRE54G Wireless-G Range Expander (available at Digital Fusion).

2 Select the optimum location for the repeater.

3 If it is available, use the device's configuration button to let you connect to your home network automatically.

4 If you use Wireless Encryption Protocol (WEP), use the configuration wizard on the CD that comes with the device to configure the device manually.

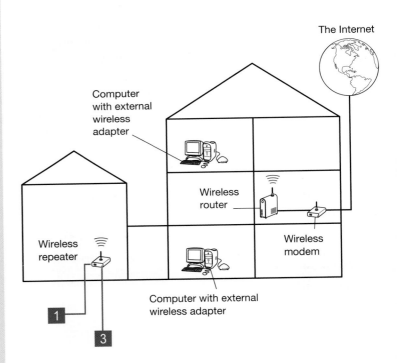

Did you know? ❓

A rose is a rose is a rose is a rose. But you might see a repeater referred to as a wireless range extender, wireless range expander or signal booster. Another big advantage of using a repeater rather than a second access point is the fact that the repeater is designed to communicate wirelessly with the primary access point. In other words, you don't need to go through the time and expense of installing Ethernet cable or home power adapters.

Because the average home network consists of multiple components and extends from room to room or floor to floor, a variety of problems can occur. Some of the following tasks are based on situations I've encountered myself. I'm particularly happy to pass along solutions that I hit upon only after trying different alternatives. I hope they will help save you time and trouble when you need to troubleshoot your own network setup.

Clearing interference from cordless phones

▶

When I first got my wireless router, everything worked fine until I received a phone call or attempted to make a phone call. My 'land line' had a wireless handset, and it transmitted on the same 2.4 GHz frequency that the router was using. The solution was not to exchange the router for a new one but to obtain a new cordless phone handset.

1 Try operating your current phone with its antenna lowered (if it is retractible) to see if that eliminates interference.

2 Purchase a telephone that operates on the 5.8 GHz frequency band, such as the one shown, or the Uniden TRU9465 with two handsets, available from **http://www.amazon.co.uk**.

?

Did you know?

You might not encounter the interference problem with every router and every cordless handset. Only routers that use the 802.11b and 802.11g protocols operate on the 2.4 GHz frequency.

When I visited a friend's house and asked to use her home wireless Internet connection, she told me she was having trouble getting online anywhere but in the kitchen. Since wireless routers should be able to transmit a signal through much of a typical home (if not throughout the whole house), I was curious. I discovered that the router had been placed directly beneath the microwave oven, and the oven was apparently interfering with it.

For your information

Baby monitors, garage door openers, home automation devices and other devices that emit wireless radio signals can potentially interfere with your wireless router signal.

Avoiding interference from other home appliances

1. Make sure your wireless router isn't adjacent to microwaves or other appliances that emit radio waves.

2. Try to mount the router as close to the ceiling of the room as you can get; this will help eliminate interference and transmit the signal further.

13

Tracking interference from other networking equipment

When attending a conference, several attendees attempted to get online using the organisation's wireless network. The signal was intermittent – we would be online for 10–15 minutes and then offline for a few minutes. When we reported the situation to the network administrator, he tracked the problem to the room full of computer and electrical equipment. The router was just inches from another wireless access point that was apparently interfering with it.

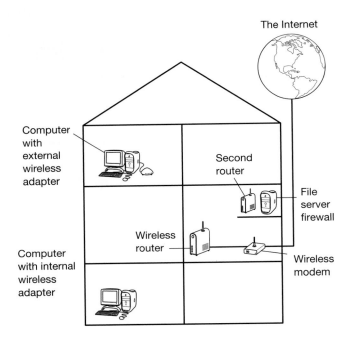

If you have routers or other networking equipment close to one another in the same room, separate them as much as possible.

Suppose you've investigated all of the internal sources of interference mentioned above, and your wireless network connection is still functioning poorly. The problem may be outside your property. **In densely populated areas, it's not unusual for wireless signals from one person's home network to penetrate a neighbour's home and interfere with their own wireless network.**

Tracking problems outside your home

1 Change the channel.

2 Click **Save Settings**.

3 If that doesn't work, consult your neighbour and try to use channels that won't interfere with each other: channels 1, 6 and 11 are unlikely to interfere with each other, for instance.

13

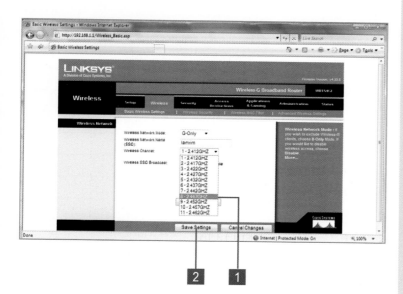

Tracking problems outside your home (cont.)

Table 17.1 Wireless channels in Europe (2.4 GHz range)	
Channel	Frequency range
Channel 1	2399.5 MHz–2424.5 MHz
Channel 2	2404.5 MHz–2429.5 MHz
Channel 3	2409.5 MHz–2434.5 MHz
Channel 4	2414.5 MHz–2439.5 MHz
Channel 5	2419.5 MHz–2444.5 MHz
Channel 6	2424.5 MHz–2449.5 MHz
Channel 7	2429.5 MHz–2454.5 MHz
Channel 8	2434.5 MHz–2459.5 MHz
Channel 9	2439.5 MHz–2464.5 MHz
Channel 10	2444.5 MHz–2469.5 MHz
Channel 11	2449.5 MHz–2474.5 MHz
Channel 12	2454.5 MHz–2479.5 MHz
Channel 13	2459.5 MHz–2484.5 MHz

?

Did you know?

In the US, users have 11 wireless channels from which to choose. In the UK and other parts of Europe, 13 channels are available.

Sometimes, the problem isn't hardware, software or even your neighbours. It has to do with the environment. You've probably noticed that it's difficult to go online when you're outdoors and you don't have a clear line of sight to the sky. Heavy rain and other severe weather can also wreak havoc with your home wireless connection.

Tracking other environmental issues

1 If you think your wireless connection has broken due to the weather, you can connect your computer to your router using an Ethernet cable.

13

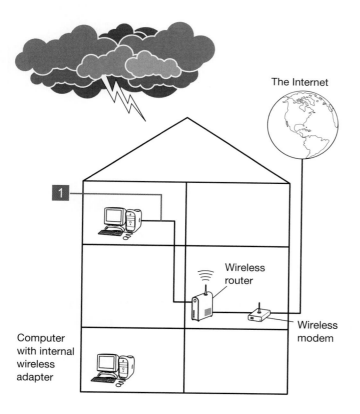

The Internet

Wireless router

Wireless modem

Computer with internal wireless adapter

For your information

You might consider a Power Over Ethernet adapter as an alternative to wireless in this situation, but home plug objects would be risky due to the chance of lightning strikes.

Tracing firewall problems

If you are unable to connect to the Internet from a particular computer, make sure your firewall program isn't blocking it. If you haven't renewed your firewall's annual subscription fee, it might be blocking you from connecting to the Internet. (This happened to me when I was using an older version of Norton Internet Security.)

1 Turn off your firewall by right-clicking the icon in the System Tray and choosing **Pause Protection**, **Disable** or a similar command from the context menu.

2 If the connection problem disappears when you pause the firewall, open the program by double-clicking its icon.

3 Click **Firewall**.

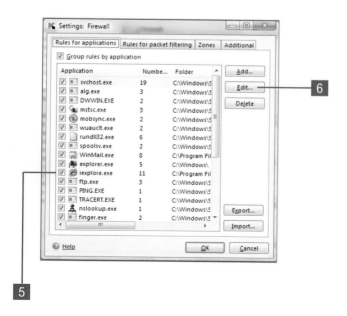

4 Click the option that allows you to review applications that access the Internet. In the case of this program, click **Settings** (your own program's options will vary).

5 Scan the list of programs that are allowed to access the Internet. Make sure your web browser of choice is among them. Click **iexplore.exe** to check Internet Explorer.

6 Click **Edit**.

13

Tracing firewall problems (cont.)

7 Highlight **Internet Explorer HTTP Activity**, which describes web browsing.

8 Make sure outbound traffic is allowed on port 80, the port used for basic web surfing.

9 Click **OK**.

10 If the problem is that your computers cannot 'see' one another on the network, turn off each machine's firewall, one at a time, to see if the problem is resolved. If the problem disappears when you turn one firewall off, that's the cause.

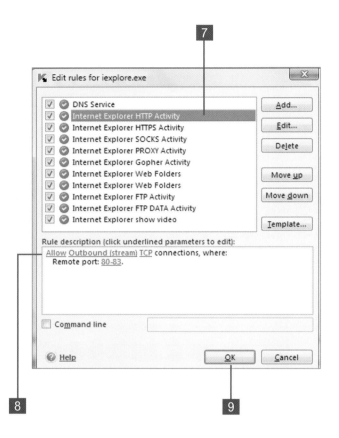

For your information

If turning off firewalls doesn't resolve the problem, you can also turn off network adapters one by one to see if that enables your computers to connect to one another.

If one or more of your computers slows to a crawl or is non-functional, it may be telling you that it's sick. In fact, it may be infected with viruses and/or spyware. As I've mentioned before, when you connect multiple computers to the Internet by means of a home network, you need to protect all of those computers from spyware and viruses. When a computer has 24/7 access to the Internet, it becomes a target for hackers who want to plant malicious programs on it. They don't necessarily want to steal personal information (though this is a possibility); they want to take over the machine and use it to send spam e-mail or launch attacks on websites.

◀ Checking for spyware and viruses

1 Go to the Lavasoft website (**http://www.lavasoft.com**) and download a free version of Ad-Aware SE Personal.

2 Click **Start** to scan your system for spyware.

1

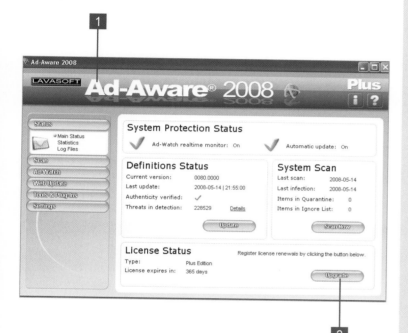

2

13

Checking for spyware and viruses (cont.)

3 Choose a scan mode.

4 Click **Scam** to start the scan.

5 When the scan is complete, click **Finish**.

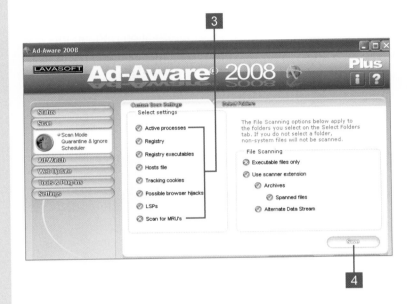

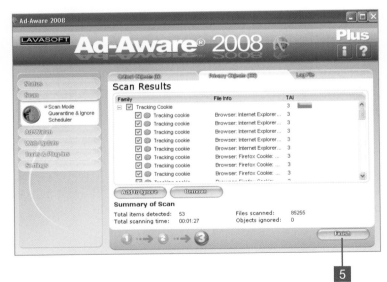

Checking for spyware and viruses (cont.)

6 Click the plus sign (+) next to each critical object to find out more about it.

7 Tick the box next to each item you want to eliminate.

8 Click **Quarantine** to place the item(s) in a protected area of your computer where they cannot harm other files.

9 Click **Finish** to permanently remove the objects you selected.

13

For your information

Ad-Aware is a good starter program, but it is no substitute for a full-fledged virus scanner that is updated regularly and automatically protects each of your computers that have access to the Internet and to each other.

If your network adapter won't connect

If you have an external network card/adapter that you plug into your laptop and it cannot connect to the Internet, the problem may be that you aren't receiving a 'routable' IP address from your router by means of Dynamic Host Configuration Protocol (DHCP). (A routable IP address is one that can be used to surf the Internet from 'behind' a router.) The clue is that your adapter's IP address begins with 169.254.

1 To check your adapter's IP address, click **Start** and type **cmd**.

2 When the cmd command prompt application appears, press **Enter**.

3 At the command prompt, type **ipconfig /all**, and press **Enter**.

4 Check the current IP address; if it begins with 192.168, DHCP is functioning properly. If it begins with 169.254, DHCP is not functioning, possibly because the computer is not connected. If it is not connected, do the following.

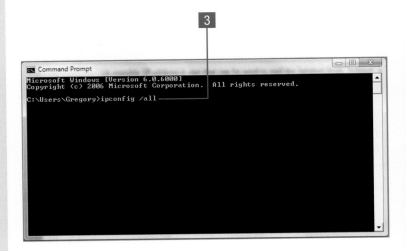

For your information

If your network adapter has an IP address that begins with 169.254 rather than 192.168, that means it probably isn't connected to the router. The 169.254.x.x set of IP addresses is reserved for Microsoft software testing and is not intended for surfing the Internet. The 192.168.x.x series of addresses is for internal use on a local network, too, but they can be routed to the router, which connects to the Web using its public IP address.

5 Verify that the status lights on the back of the network card are the proper colour. See your network card documentation for what the different colours mean. If they aren't the right colour, there are at least five possibilities:

- The cable is broken.
- The cable is not firmly connected at both ends.
- The port on the hub or router is broken. Try plugging the network cable into a different port on the hub or router.
- The network card is not functioning properly.
- The cable is of the wrong kind.

13

Disabling firewalls when networking printers

▶

At some point when you're operating your home network, you will probably want to share a printer. The most common setup calls for the printer to be connected to one of your home computers with a USB cable. The computer, in turn, is plugged into one of the ports on your router. If your computer isn't able to 'see' the printer even though everything else appears to be functioning properly, you can troubleshoot by disabling any firewall programs you have running.

1 First, disable the firewall on the PC to which the printer is attached.

2 If that doesn't work, disable the firewall on the PC that is attempting to access the network printer.

3 Let the computer automatically configure the printer. If it does not automatically configure the printer when you attempt to print, open the Control Panel and double-click **Printers**.

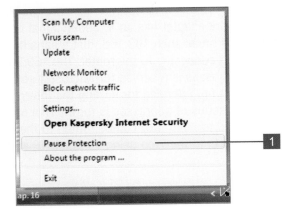

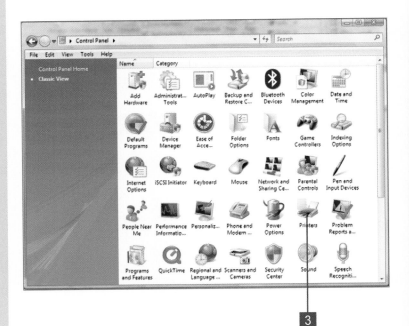

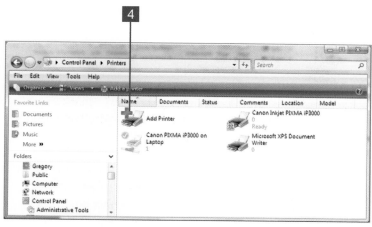

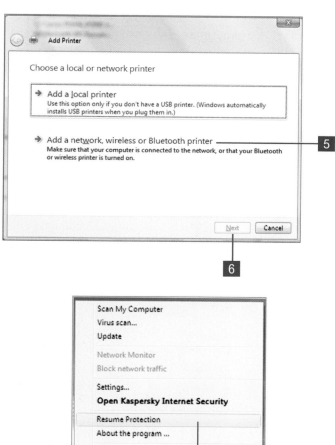

4 Add a printer.

5 Click **Add a network, wireless or Bluetooth printer**.

6 Click **Next** and follow the steps shown in subsequent screens.

7 Re-enable the firewalls and check to see whether or not the printer is now visible on the network. It should be accessible once it has been configured.

13

What is in a wireless channel?

Your wireless channel is something you probably won't think about until you encounter problems on the network: say, your computer is periodically disconnected from the network or your network performance slows down dramatically.

The problem might be caused by interference from other devices using the same frequency as your wireless router. The wireless networks being used by your neighbours might also interfere. The most common wireless standards, 802.11b and 802.11g, use the 2.4 GHz frequency range. The key word is range: this isn't a single frequency, but a signal range that is subdivided into smaller bands or 'channels'.

When you first configure your router, one of the channels is selected by default. This channel, however, isn't necessarily the best one for your needs. You can 'change the channel' (much as you would on a television) and get some improvement. The channels in the wireless frequency range overlap, so they don't have to be exactly the same. However, your network will work best if your router and network adapters all use the same channel for wireless communications.

Jargon buster

Ad-hoc network – a network in which computers or other devices are temporarily connected for a specific purpose.

Bluetooth – this protocol is used for data communications in Personal Area Networks (PANs), which include handhelds, mobile phones, laptops and other devices that support Bluetooth.

Client – a computer that connects via a network to another computer that has been designated a file server.

DHCP – system software that dynamically assigns network addresses to computers that are connected to one another.

DNS (Domain Name Service) – a system that uses recognisable aliases like speakeasy.net or pearson.com in place of hard-to-remember IP addresses.

DNS server – a computer provided by your ISP that enables you to access websites by translating their domain names into IP addresses.

Ethernet – a high-speed networking technology used in local area networks to connect computers, modems and other devices by means of Ethernet cables.

Hub – a network device that contains multiple ports to enable computers to plug into it with Ethernet cables. Hubs can only send or receive information at one time; they cannot send and receive simultaneously.

IEEE (Institute of Electrical and Electronics Engineers) – creates wireless standards for network communications.

IP address – a number that uniquely identifies a computer on the Internet using Internet Protocol (IP). IP version 4 uses four-part numbers – four numbers connected by dots. A newer version, IPv6, uses six-part numbers.

LAN (local area network) – a group of interconnected computers located in a small area, such as a house, office or single building.

MAC Address – short for Media Access Control address, a complex series of numbers that identifies a network adapter.

Modem – hardware that connects a computer or other digital device to a network, such as the Internet, through phone lines or cable systems.

NIC (network interface card) – hardware that plugs into a laptop or desktop computer and that enables the computer to exchange data with a network.

Patch cable – a specific type of CAT-5 cable used to connect computers temporarily, as in a hotel room.

PCI (Peripheral Component Interconnect) – a standard for connecting peripheral devices to personal computers.

PCMCIA – a type of card that uses the Personal Computer Memory Card International Association standard for data storage and transfer. PCMCIA cards are typically used by laptops for wireless network access and other functions.

Peer-to-peer network – a type of network in which there is no central file server, but rather each computer serves as a file server in its own right.

Personal area network – a group of devices that communicate using the Bluetooth protocol.

Phoneline – a networking system that uses existing phone lines to carry data from one computer to another or to and from the Internet.

Powerline – a networking system that uses existing power wiring used to bring electrical power to all of your appliances to carry data from one computer to another or to and from the Internet.

Router – network devices that act as controllers, directing and forwarding packets to different computers or other network devices.

Server – a network computer equipped with software and/or hardware that enables the distribution of information to client computers.

Switch – a network device that has the ability to identify the destination of the data that comes to it. Switches can send and receive information at the same time.

TCP/IP – a set of protocols that enable host and client computers to send and receive information across a network such as the Internet. TCP stands for Transmission Control Protocol, and IP stands for Internet Protocol.

Wired – a network that uses Ethernet, phoneline or powerline technology to physically connect devices by means of cables.

Wireless – a network that uses a wireless modem to transmit digital data to a computer or other device (such as a mobile phone or PDA) without cables.

Troubleshooting guide